I0202886

YOU'RE **WORTH MORE** TO GOD
THAN ALL THE PEOPLE
WHO THINK YOU ARE WORTHLESS.

*"If God waited on people to become perfect
before He anointed them
to preach, teach, lead or minister,
there would never be anyone worthy,
and the work would never get done.*

*God uses willing vessels, with weaknesses,
so His strength, power, and anointing,
can shine through,
and He can get the glory!"*

Keith Hammond

Success After Setback

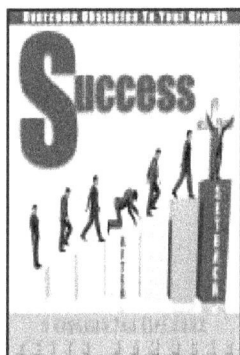

Overcoming Obstacles to your Growth

Cover Layout and Interior Design: Keith Hammond

Lessons For Life Books
PUBLISHERS

L E S S O N S F O R L I F E B O O K S . C O M

Unless otherwise indicated, any and all Scripture quotations are from the Holy Bible, King James version. All Rights Reserved.

LessonsForLifeBooks.com

IMPRINT A Lessons For Life Book

Success After Setback

Overcoming Obstacles
To Your Growth

© 2014 by
Keith Hammond
is published by
Lessons for Life Books, Inc.
1715 W. 7th Street #16148
St Paul, MN 55116

No part of this book may be reproduced or utilized in any for or by any means, electronic or mechanical, including photocopying, recording, or by any information storage or retrieval system, without permission in writing from the Publisher.

Inquiries should be addressed in writing to:
Lessons For Life Books
1715 W. 7th Street #16148
St Paul, MN 55116
or by email to:
permissionrequest@LessonsForLifeBooks.com

ISBN-13: 978-1-938588-55-6
Library of Congress Control Number: 2012915341
Printed in the U.S.A.

Dedication

God Almighty,
I give you all the glory, honor, and praise for all that you have done
and still do in, to, and through, my life.
Thank you for Jesus Christ and the Holy Spirit,
and for the redeeming power of your Love.

To my wife,
in this 29th year together,
thank you for all your prayers and patience.

To my daughters,
my Love for you goes beyond words.
Many blessings to you both.

To my grandsons,
it is a great joy
to be Blessed with your presence in our lives.

To the Hammond and Fitzpatrick families,
I pray that you will unite arm in arm one day
and allow yourselves to be encircled by
the healing power of God's Love.

To Pastor Arthur Agnew,
only God could know how grateful I am,
for the 10 years you stood by my side.
Your training, teaching, and telling, will always be with me.

Acknowledgement

There are may people who at some point and time of my life,
made a measurable impact, whether good or bad,
I'm thankful for your input into me.
It helped God prune, grow and mature me in more ways,
than you will ever know.

God Bless You All.

Table Of Contents

*Prayer
Patience
and
Persistence
Pays*

*Using these
simple tools*

*You can
overcome
most any
setback*

~

*Keith
Hammond*

Success After Setback

Introduction 08

CHAPTER ONE **17**
Tragedy 18
Drug use 22
Drug sales.. 26
Gang affiliation 30
Fornication.. 34
CHAPTER TWO **39**
Limitless lies 40
Negative outcomes 45
Felonies 50
Victims 54
Enemies 57
CHAPTER THREE **61**
Foreclosures 62
Lawsuits 66
Judgments & Liens...................................... 70
Bankruptcy 73
Debt 76
CHAPTER FOUR **81**
Burned bridges 82
Blacklist 86
Surveillance... 90
Sabotage 94
CHAPTER FIVE **99**
Bouncing Back 100
Books 123
Bookstore 126
Cafe` 130
CD 133
Church 136
CHAPTER SIX **139**
Building New Bridges.................................. 140
Taking Risks.. 143
Support Groups 146
Summary Pages 152
Closing Thoughts 156

Introduction

I've been through some things. Many things. I've been through things that most people couldn't survive, recover from, or want to even continue going after experiencing it.

The night my mom passed, a relative molested me. I've had guns placed at my temple. I've been in a three-way crossfire and if God's hand were not on us could have killed me, my wife, and our kids.

I've done things I regret, don't understand, and get sickened every time I think about how an intelligent, gifted, creative, and naturally athletic African-American male, could ever allow the things of this world, temptations that so easily beset us, and works of the devil to ever play a part in some of the hurtful things I've done to others.

The ministry God entrusted to me was conceived, nurtured, and birthed into manifestation while going through the setbacks you see listed in these pages. Until later in life, I never realized that it was all part of God's process of maturing me. I finally recognized, that in spite of most of these things being self-inflicted, I gave the devil permission just by my own actions, and attitude. I thank God that "All Things Work Together For Good to Them That Love God, Who Are The Called According To His Purpose." Knowing this, helped me understand that God is still in control. This, is the story of how God sees me, even when I couldn't look at myself.

Success After Setback tells the story of how I've been able to overcome setbacks in my life such as:

+ Tragedy

+ Drug use

+ Drug sales

+ Gang affiliation

+ Fornication

+ Limitless lies

+ Negative outcomes

+ Felonies

+ Victims

+ Enemies

+ Foreclosures

+ Lawsuits

+ Judgments & Liens

+ Bankruptcies

+ Debt

+ Burned bridges

+ Blacklist

+ Surveillance

+ Sabotage

Other things can be added to this list. I had to overcome them in order to get back in God's will so He could use me for His purpose. Without having God's will to help me, the statement in a powerful Gospel song, which says: "I should have been dead and gone, but Lord you let me live on," would not be true.

Have you ever been to prison?
Do you know anyone who has?

Have you ever been in debt?
Do you know anyone who has?

Have you ever lost your home?
Do you know anyone who has?

Have you ever been sued?
Do you know anyone who has?

Have you ever been in the news?
Do you know anyone who has?

Has your marriage ever been in trouble?
Do you know anyone who has?

Have you ever lost your job?
Do you know anyone who has?

Have you ever been without income for a long period of time?
Do you know anyone who has?

Have you ever been accused of something you didn't do?
Do you know anyone who has?

Have you ever wanted to just give up and end it all?
Do you know anyone who has?

These are just some of the things I've been through. Yes, all of them, and a laundry list of others. I wrote this book to help whoever reads it understand that there can ALWAYS be success after setback, IF, you're willing to let God pick you up, dust you off, and place you back on the path to try again. Most people give up after failing once. I never have. I'm determined, resilient, and purposed to do some good in my life, and God gave me dozens of chances to get it right.

Why was I given so many chances? Simple. I understand what it says in Proverbs 24:16 that, "For a just man falleth seven times, and riseth up again" and Luke 12:48: "For unto whomsoever much is given, of him shall be much required." Both speak directly to my life.

I recognized that in spite of any demonic influences, generational curses, altered courses, and even self-inflicted setbacks, that God forgives and forgets. Isaiah 43:25 says, "I, even I, am He that blotteth out thy transgressions for mine own sake, and will not remember thy sins." These scriptures laid the foundation, the pathways, and the course for me to return back to God, after waddling in the mud of the mess I'd made of my life.

MY NAME IS KEITH HAMMOND. For decades I lived life in what I perceived as a grey area between right and wrong. There is no grey area. I did right half the time. I did wrong half the time. I knew this imbalance was directly related to me rebelling against my parents for dying. My Mom passed in 1972, my Dad in 1980. I was age 17, left in a drug and gang infested neighborhood to fend for myself. The day my dad passed I heard God's voice. Because I ignored it, the next 11 years were pure hell. In 1991, I heard God's voice again. It was after He spared my life in a three-way crossfire designed to kill me, and could have also taken the life of my wife, and kids. Although I moved my family to another state, I didn't leave the grey area. I didn't know how. Leaving the atmosphere did nothing for my attitude or actions.

In 1996, I gave my life to Christ, joined a church, and started partially living for God. I still lived in a grey area but I was willing to surrender, and let God change my life, so He started working on me.

God sent me to jail for six months. The system He created called "Corrections" is a place to send people who have behavior within them that is not like Him, and thus, needs to be 'corrected'. When I was released, I came out and went right back to the grey area. Years later He sent me back and I still didn't stop. I didn't know how. My rebellion had a source that until I owned up to it, exposed it, and told the truth about it, wouldn't go away. That rebellion was the anger I still held from my past. That unforgiveness kept me in bondage as long as I held on to it and refused to let it go.

MY PERSONAL LIFE

Fast forward to 2012, 16 years after giving my life to Christ. On the surface, I lived in the comfort of a 28 year relationship and marriage; had raised two well-adjusted daughters ages 28 and 23; was guiding two grandsons ages 6 and 4; celebrated 21 years of sobriety; and 16 years of using my gifts, skills, talents, abilities, memory, knowledge and resources to help edify the Body of Christ and many ministries. I take tremendous pride in these accomplishments in spite of the reality of living with a tumor next to my solar plexus most of my adult life; dealing with the tragedy and scars from the many deaths around me in my childhood; and the stress that not having income for over three years placed on my marriage and my family.

MY PROFESSIONAL LIFE

On the flip side of the accomplishments, I was a man who took what I've been blessed with to use for good, and manipulated situations to my advantage to get money. As a result, my past is littered with many victims, negative outcomes, restitution, lawsuits, judgments, and a ton of debt. I've always managed to build success after setbacks, including self-inflicted ones, but this time had to be different because it was my last chance. I knew that if I did not walk into God's calling on my life it would be my last chance to do so.

I continue to grieve for my parents, because I don't have them around any longer to tell how I feel. To let them know how badly I suffered, how much it hurt, and how alone and abandoned I felt. On top of all that, to tell them that the night that my mom died, my own relative molested me.

Because I couldn't take my pain out on my parents, I took it out on any and everyone who I got into any kind of relationship with. The relationships started, but I always held it in my mind, that before they got a chance to leave me, abandon me, or hurt me, I would hurt them first, and I did.

This destructive behavior had to stop somewhere. I knew the only way was to own up to it, expose it, tell the truth about it, be transparent through it, and be willing to talk about every part of it, including and especially the parts I didn't want anyone else to know.

I lived with separation anxiety all those years and it haunted me. Because I'm exposing it, telling the truth about it, and sharing what I went through as testimony, I'm able to deal with it. I still live with the hurt, pain, anger, unresolved grief, and other issues behind the death of both my parents. Because I've finally forgiven them and thankful for the time they were in my life and I'm now able to cope.

In my personal life, I've been voted Saint of the Year; Hardest Working Father of the Year; and Hardest Working Church Member. I've accomplished things in the church that it would take ten people to do, because of the varied and numerous gifts God has given me.

In my professional life, no one trusted me and I couldn't outlive, outrun, or out-explain my past.

These two dynamics were at opposite ends of the spectrum and in total odds against each other. One was flesh, the other spirit. I had to surrender to the stronger of the two, to get people to trust me again; restore the relationships; get completely back in God's will so He could use me as a willing vessel to give my testimony so that others could be helped. It wasn't easy but I kept the Faith that it could be done. God has forgiven and restored others, so I knew my time was coming. The moment God saw "true surrender" in my heart doors to start over began to open. I got offered jobs; I started paying restitution; I was asked to be a mentor; my books were published and so on.

How do you kill off a Goliath in your life, if the giant you're fighting against, is you?

This is testimony of how God gave me success after setback,
and He can do the same for you.

Success
After
Setback

Chapter
One

THE PROCESS

THE SUCCESS

THE SETBACK
~TRAGEDY~

Most people experience tragedy in their lives at some point. Whether it's the death of loved ones, violation of your physical body, or mental anguish from the devastation of war, something happens in the lives of most people. These incidents often cause us to retreat into stages of depression, anger, guilt, and other states of mind that sometimes preclude addiction, and/or rebellion and other destructive behavior.

In my life, there were ten tragedies that occurred from age 8 to age 18. Ten tragedies in ten years. They brought on grief, anger, depression, frustration, loneliness, feelings of abandonment, confusion, and a whole range of other emotions. Even some misplaced ones that I never dealt with because I didn't know how. I was too young. In my neighborhood in that era, therapy was not an option and something most of the folks in my community had never even heard of.

My autobiography is titled, *"Ten Years Ten Tears."* I wrote it to help peel off layers of unresolved grief I carried most of my life.

Underneath the layers, you will witness me emerge into the person that God used those ten tragedies in ten years and other incidents in my later years to mold and shape me into the minister He designed, gifted, trained and matured me to be. The man I am today.

THE CHALLENGE

The challenge to overcome tragedy in one's life can be quite difficult if you let it. The major challenge can be letting go of the guilt and feeling of 'it's my fault' when dealing with the aftermath. Guilt can produce or bring about a significant amount of self-blame. If guilt and self-blame are allowed to persist, individually and collectively they can extend far above the normal levels.

Guilt, in itself, is a major challenge to overcome. How does one overcome the feeling of guilt in tragic circumstances? It's not an easy answer. Disconnecting and deliverance from guilt requires an examination of self-worth that needs to be joined together with whatever self-esteem exists in order to defeat guilt. In my own life, again, there were ten tragedies in ten years. I valued my own life enough to know that I had to carry on. When I finally realized I had something to offer, I began to give God glory, thereby releasing the guilt to Him, because it was too heavy a burden for me to carry.

Feelings of self-blame manifested in a way that I didn't see coming or recognize. Why did it surface? Simple: It came from me asking myself varied questions such as, "Why is this happening to me"? "Is there anything I should or could have done"? And the answers were just as simple: "It's not happening to you." "There is nothing you should have or could have done." In fact, the same answer could be used to sum up the myriad of other 'self-blame' questions that surfaced. That answer is: "This tragic situation isn't about you."

I had to realize that any tragedy that happened to my relatives or people that were close to me was not my fault and had nothing to do with me at all. They were tragedies that were either brought on by old-age, sickness from disease of some sort, or death at the hands of someone who had no regard for the life of that individual, in spite of the fact that they were related to me. This realization, used as a simple response to the onset of self-blame, *was the very solution needed to overcome the challenge.*

THE PROCESS

The process of overcoming any challenge related to feelings of guilt or self-blame is as simple as letting your spirit answer the questions your flesh will ask. As humans, our emotional strength comes from a solid foundation in and relationship with God. That strength and fortitude can often be weakened by the emotional attachment to the people involved in the tragedy. The deaths that took place in my life started at such an early age for me, I never had time, was taught, or learned how to deal with the grief behind it.

Grief unresolved can become guilt. Mine did. I was searching for answers to what was happening around me that no one would talk about. Because no one ever said a word to me about it, I believed it was my fault. I didn't realize until I was well into my late thirties that their silence was a way to protect me and it also signified that my input into the situation wasn't needed or welcomed.

Moving past any feelings of guilt, self-blame or grief did not happen overnight. It took years of prayer. The most significant tool that helped me through the process was writing my autobiography.

+ **Writing** it down forced me to think about it.
+ **Thinking** about it required me to relive it.
+ **Reliving** it brought it to the surface where I had to face it.
+ **Facing** it ushered me into being delivered from it.

Writing my autobiography was therapeutic. It was freeing. It was healing. And I wouldn't change the process for anything in the world.

THE SUCCESS

The success that has taken place since being freed from the emotional attachment to the tragedies that occurred in my past is immeasurable.

Examples include being courageous and bold enough to stand and participate as one of the two ministers that presided over and conducted the funeral of one of my nephews where dozens of my family members attended. When I sang, much of my family was in tears. Prior to being freed from the tragedy in my past, I couldn't even attend a funeral, let alone conduct one. While serving 12 years as the right hand to the pastor at a Baptist church in Minneapolis, God used him to help me get over my fear of death. I'm grateful to God for helping me and to Pastor Agnew for standing in the gap.

THE SETBACK
~DRUG USE~

My mom passed in 1972. I was 9 years old. That same night I was molested by a relative. It took me four years to start working to battle back from the devastation of that day. Once I came out of my shell, I excelled at academics and sports because I had found two outstanding avenues to channel the anger. This newfound band-aid did not cover the scars for long because just eight short years after the death of my mom, my dad died. In 1980, he went to the doctor accompanied by a family friend, and never came home. I was 17.

Until his death, my dad protected me from many things, including drug use. Using drugs came easy after that. It seemed almost natural. I soon learned that it wasn't. It was actually the devil's way of keeping me distracted from hearing and heeding the call God has on my life.

My drug of choice was marijuana. It is a hallucinogen that keeps your mind clouded, and your senses dulled to the point that reality itself becomes a blur. Back then, drug dealers and users were starting to experiment with adding additional substances such as PCP, on top of the marijuana as if it wasn't strong enough already.

I know people whose minds didn't survive the experiment. I know people who died from it. Even though I was subjecting my mind and body to it, God protected me.

THE CHALLENGE

When the devil knows there is a calling on your life he uses every tool at his disposal to try and set you back. He throws darts and circumstances in your path to keep you distracted and off course. When I began to use drugs, the worse it got. The more I used the deeper I fell. The deeper I fell the harder it was to quit. My marijuana use graduated to opium in the form of sprinkling hash on the weed. That lasted six years. In 1987, for the entire summer, opium was replaced by cocaine. I had never heard of it, but my marijuana customers were asking for it. So I found it and started selling it. And because I'm the type to never give anyone else something I haven't tried myself, I tried it.

That was one of the biggest mistakes in my life because trying it up my nose, escalated to doing it the way other people did it, which was to cook it, place it on a screen on the top of the stem of a glass pipe, and smoke it. The only words I can come up with to describe this activity is stupidity and craziness. It was hellish. By the time I realized it, my crack habit had taken over my sanity, my decisions, my life.

I'm forever grateful to my wife who would not give up on me. She prayed, and prayed, and prayed. While I was in hotel rooms smoking crack, she would be in there in tears, praying for me. At the end of the summer of 1987, I was so deep that I had lost about 40 pounds. When I looked in the mirror I no longer saw myself staring back. I needed help and my wife's prayers kicked into high gear.

God used the very thing I was most afraid of to wake me up. My biggest fear was rats. Chicago is full of them. One evening when I was smoking crack in the basement of a rental townhome, I went upstairs to the second floor, forgetting I had left the basement door open. When I came back downstairs, there was a rat standing up on his hind legs, positioned between me and the crack. Long story short, I left the crack and the rat in the basement, walked out the front door of that townhome and didn't return. I was free. Just like that. My high wore off. I never saw that basement again. I paid some movers to go get my stuff out of that townhome and I never went back. I don't know if the rat smoked the crack and I didn't care.

THE PROCESS

The process of me overcoming drug use is most likely vastly different than most people. During my crack habit, my wife was willing to stay next to me, pray for me, and protect me. She saw that something had taken over her husband's mind and body and she was not willing to give up without a fight. She recognized that this was a spiritual battle that I brought upon myself, and because I had invited it into my life, I was unable to fight it or even have the sense to do so. My deliverance came through prayer and fear.

Through others I've since counseled through addictions I've learned that the first step is admitting you have a problem. Denial is the enemy. Admittance is the armor. Remember, truth is the only thing that can set you free.

Once you're willing to admit that a substance is a problem in your life, you have to be ready to stop. If you're not, you'll keep lying to yourself and to others, while you continue to subject your body and mind to the poison that is drugs and alcohol. If you allow them to, both will take control of your life until you're ready to take it back. Once you're ready to get free from the bondage and hold that these substances can have on your life, the process may not be as easy as it was for me to stop. I believe my wife's prayers reached Heaven, and God in his infinite wisdom, dispatched a rat to serve as a wake up call to me. It worked. God can use something just as simple for you too, but you have to be willing to walk away and say enough is enough. I was. You can too.

Once you're willing to *admit* that you have a problem, prayer brings hope in. When hope starts to work, it invites mercy and grace in to cover and protect you. Once they're in place, surrender knocks on the door of your heart. In order to open it you have to confess that you've sinned. Confession leads to repentance, which calls on forgiveness to usher in redemption. Then healing starts and *deliverance* steps in. So, from admittance to deliverance, there are steps to take and they are well worth it.

THE SUCCESS

My success is evident today. My wife and I are in our 30th year. My kids are 29 & 24 and neither was affected by my drug use. I've been in ministry 16 years and continue to help people get beyond addiction.

THE SETBACK
~DRUG SALES~

After my dad passed away in 1980 I immediately became the next target for the gang in my neighborhood. I knew them because I lived on the block with the leaders. They quickly gave me the ultimatum to do or die. I chose to join, and they initiated me by beating me as much as I could stand until I fought back. One of their activities was drug sales so it became my activity. I had a relative that dealt in large quantities so I became a buyer of the heavier weights, processed it, and prepared it for sale on the street. I sold drugs until I moved away from the block, and changed my life.

During the time I was selling drugs I was robbed at gunpoint twice, had friends steal drugs and other items from me several times, gave away drugs to women who were willing to sleep with me for it, and also used my share of the inventory. I had so much money from the drug sales that I didn't care either way.

Drug sales kept me distracted from walking into God's calling on my life. It was a setback that lasted from 1980 to 1991. Even though I never got caught, I know many people who went to jail for decades from selling. I know many people who died from refusing to give up their stash to those who were trying to take it. And, I know many who died from using. Drugs took over our neighborhood and destroyed lives. Many people who fell into this trap never escaped.

THE CHALLENGE

Overcoming the challenge of being a drug dealer typically only comes when the quick and easy money is replaced with another form of gain. My gain, was meeting the woman who would eventually become my wife. The challenge to get out of that life came through an incident that almost took my life, hers, and our kids. We got caught in a crossfire where three men were shooting at me because I wasn't supposed to be in their turf, even though I was only there to let my wife visit her mom. Getting shot at for me was nothing. It had happened before. Being responsible for almost getting my wife and kids killed, changed me.

That was the day 'enough is enough' slapped me square in the face. I waited until later that day, and made a way for my wife to go back to her mom's house, without me. I got on the freeway and went 90 miles away to Milwaukee where I was working on projects and getting a presence established there. I went there to cool down so I wouldn't retaliate, and to hide in case the shooters were still looking for me.

After a couple of weeks I called my wife at her mom's house and told her to pack a couple of bags of clothes. I packed my clothes in the trunk, drove to get her and the kids, said our good-byes, and hit the highway. I left everything behind. Drugs, money, people. I left that life as quickly as I had started it. Me, my wife, and our kids drove to and settled in Minneapolis, which we knew nothing about. It was a place for us to start over, and we did.

THE PROCESS

The process of getting out of the life of being a drug dealer was an event that both saved me from eventual death and changed my life. Getting caught in a crossfire that did not harm me, is the process I believe God used to push me toward the place where He had ordered my steps so that I would walk into my calling. The process of getting out of drug sales may be different for you. Many of the young men I ran with in those days ended up dead or in jail. I believe my path was different because of the calling on my life and the fact that from age 16, I was always willing to walk into it. I got sidetracked because of the many circumstances I faced from losing both my parents and the rebellion that followed.

I believe that if our family had been given the support from people in the church that we so desperately needed following the death of my mom in 1972 and my dad in 1980, I would not have ended up on the streets. In retrospect, I wouldn't change anything I experienced because those trials and tribulations helped me to build character. Getting shot at because you've entered a rival gang's turf; or getting chased by a gang because you're buying drugs in their hood, to go sell outside their hood, has a way of building character each and every time you find yourself still alive to look in the mirror the next day. Again, your process for getting out of the game may be different, but I highly recommend you get out before you end up dead, in jail, or worse, such as being paralyzed for life because a bullet with someone else's name on it, hit you instead.

THE SUCCESS

Having success after years of dealing drugs can be as simple as still being alive to tell your story. It most certainly is true in my own life.

God saves us to serve. He saves us from bullets, beatings, and burial, in order to be useful to Him in the church and in the ministry by being living witnesses equipped to minister to others through our testimony. He wants us to help others get through what He has already brought us through.

My success since living life as a drug dealer is a miracle, and God's blessing is evident:

+ 29+ year relationship with my wife, and an empty nest.
+ 29 & 24 year old kids with professional careers.
+ 8 & 6 year old grandsons & two more grandkids on the way.
+ Never went to jail for drugs.
+ Never caught a bullet.
+ Survived two major beatings.
+ Numerous degrees and certifications with more to come.
+ Author of dozens of books that cover many genres.
+ 16+ years in church leadership and active ministry.
+ Doctorate in Organizational Leadership [expected 2014].
+ Owner of Lessons For Life Books publishing company.
+ Owner of Books 'N Tea Bookstore/Cafe`.
+ Founder/Pastor of Gospel and Grace Christian Church.

...This is a short list. God willing, there's still more to come.

THE SETBACK
~GANG AFFILIATION~

After my dad passed away in 1980 I immediately became the next target for the gang in my neighborhood. I knew them because I lived on the block with the leaders and played sports with them. I was somewhat better than most of them, which earned me their respect. But after my dad passed, they quickly gave me the ultimatum.

As a gang member, in addition to drug sales, I became the DJ for most of the house parties. My family home, once it was empty because my dad died, became the spot for many of the house parties.

Joining a gang, for me, replaced the family I had lost to tragedy and siblings who moved away for marriage, college, post-Vietnam, etc. Gang affiliation was one of the biggest setbacks of my life because it was another way that the devil was able to distract me from walking into the calling God has on my life.

Many members of the gang had lives worse than mine until my mom and dad passed. When these tragedies occurred in my life I felt like I was at the bottom of the scale of survivability. I knew that without family support there was no way I was going to survive some of the activity members of the gang participated in, were used to, and did in order to stay in the gang, stay healthy, and stay alive. I wasn't living any longer, just surviving. Survival became my life.

Many people in my neighborhood lost their lives back then. I count 20 just from a single thought. Some lived on my block. Others were close friends or classmates. There were more, but I lost count once I moved away. A sister and a nephew, remained in the neighborhood after I left and often kept me informed of the happenings and events such as who was having a funeral next. The same is somewhat true to this day because I still have relatives living in that neighborhood.

THE CHALLENGE

Escaping a gang is often no different than organized crime in a sense that once you're part of the family, you're always part of the family. I escaped by moving away and made it a point to not be found. I went back to visit other people and places in Chicago, but I waited 10 years to return to my block. I knew the price of leaving, and only out of respect for what I had done with my life after I left the block, did the leader of the gang grant me a pardon and allowed me to live. I explained to him that one of the women I slept with got pregnant, I had to get married, and we moved away to start a family. This was new to him because he knew me by my gang nickname and reputation as 'Casanova'. The cost of joining a gang isn't worth the end result. We hurt people; caused a tremendous amount of trouble; even cost some rival gang members their lives. But we also played sports; shot pool at the corner store; partied hard; ditched school in groups; and drank endless 40 oz. bottles of Old English, Mad Dog, and Gin & Juice bought from the liquor store my neighbor owned, chased with pounds of marijuana and many keys of cocaine.

THE PROCESS

The process of leaving the gang while still alive and able to enjoy my life took the courage to walk away and the ability to stay away. I stayed away for 10 years before I showed my face again. I still had family there, so they confirmed what I told gang leaders about me getting married, having kids, and moving out of state. The gang didn't come looking for me. I didn't return to look for them. Today, I return with their respect and have their protection while I'm there. I'm respected not for how I left, because I could have lost my life for that. I earned and keep their respect for how I still go back and never forget where I come from.

The process of leaving the gang may be different for you. It may take you doing what I did and moving away, but I've seen even that approach backfire. One of the members tried it. His mom moved him away to a farm in the south, thousands of miles away from our old neighborhood. He stayed away three years. When he came back, he was dead within a week.

Today my old neighborhood is a thousand times worse. Gangs during our day had pistols and shotguns. Today they use automatic weapons, vest penetrating bullets and worse. Things we did have no comparison to the activities of today's gangs. We lost one gang-member at a time; and sometimes only one a month. Today, drive-bys and turf wars can take the lives of handfuls at a time. Again, courage to leave to settle into marriage and family life was my escape, and it worked.

My advice is to get out when and while you can. One of my best friends from the gang (R.E.) wasn't so lucky. He lost his life during a playful scuffle with his brother over some burgers. A gun in a belt fell to the floor and discharged. Another best friend (A.A.) took a handful of pills after drinking almost a fifth of alcohol at one of our parties. He didn't wake up the next morning. To this day I don't know if it was intentional. Many others, including (E.M. & A.C.) leave memories to remind me that I could have easily been on the list of those who had their obituaries read way too soon.

THE SUCCESS

Leaving the gang on my own accord and with my life intact is my success after this setback. I'm not at all regretful of any of the life circumstances that came my way as a result of the many experiences that took place during my days of gang affiliation. It matured me in more ways than I ever received from my mom, who died when I was age 9, or my dad, who died when I was age 17.

Kids that age are supposed to receive some level of teaching, training, discipline, maturity, and other nurturing from their parents. When my parents died mine was cut short. The gang, as dark and destructive as it was helped mature me.

Each accomplishment I've achieved since making the choice to move away adds to the many positive aspects of the pages and chapters that make up my success story.

THE SETBACK
~FORNICATION~

In my early teens, I was invited into, and some would say earned, a relationship with a much older woman. It was the most significant event that elevated my ego and my self-esteem through the roof. It was another major setback. It lasted several years. The devil, along with the weakness of my flesh were definitely working in tandem to keep me distracted, again, from walking into the calling on my life.

Fornication is not funny. In fact, these days, it's downright dangerous. In those days STDs were rather commonplace. God protected me from every single one. Today, diseases are deadly. Back then, the only thing I really ever worried about was getting someone pregnant. I subsequently did, and thankfully, that transitioned into what has been and still is a relationship and marriage that will reach its 30th year in August 2014.

In retrospect, the most distracting moment of this setback occurred 'the very moment' my dad gave me my very first Bible. It had a red cover, gold leaf edges, and red letters where Christ spoke. The moment my dad handed it to me there was a knock on the front door of our family home. At the door was a girl named A.S. She had never been to my house before. I didn't know she was aware of where I lived. Out of courtesy I invited her inside. The instant she came in, she grabbed my hand leaned back against the door, and worked it down the front of her pants. She was undergarment free. Being the curious teenager I was back then, I tossed the Bible across the room to the couch. She and I left my house, went to hers, and I didn't pick up a Bible again until 17 years later.

This distraction was designed and purposed to keep me away from that Bible and eventually walking into my calling. I know it beyond any shadow of doubt. The devil knows our weaknesses. He persists to use it against us to make us fall. I fell. I wasn't even up yet, and still fell. This is part of the setback cost me 17 years that I could have been active and useful in church, ministry and service to God, and I've regretted that decision each and every day of my adult life.

THE CHALLENGE

The challenge to walk away from fornication starts with ignoring the temptation. You have to want to be in covenant with God, your wife, your kids, and those who look up to you, to remain accountable and reliable. Once you step outside this covenant and circle you are subject to the weakness of your flesh, and giving it what it wants, which is self-gratification in the form of sex. To meet this challenge head on, you must surrender to the Holy Spirit. It is the only thing within your fleshly body that is stronger than you, your mind, your will, your wants, and your actions—Period. Giving way to God's Spirit that lives in you takes practice, patience, persistence, and lots of prayer. Knowing that you can overcome any temptation prevents even moving forward into the act of fornication.

THE PROCESS

The process of preventing fornication by ignoring the temptation starts with FASTING. If you can deny your flesh food for any period of time, you can certainly turn down sex. The secret is being consistent with fasting and denying your flesh food for long periods of time. I typically fast the first three days of each month. For more intense fasts, I either do them on my own, or participate with the church. My family and I have regularly fasted together for many years and the benefits are indescribable and immeasurable.

Fasting takes willpower. You must be **will**ing to allow God's **power** to strengthen His Spirit that lives in you so it gets stronger than your flesh. His Spirit must be stronger than your flesh. That's the key. God's Spirit is obviously stronger than all humankind combined. When it's inside a human, fleshly creature, you have the free will to ignore God's Spirit and let your flesh do whatever it wants to do. Many people will tell you this is supremely dangerous.

In my book titled, '*Transform Your Schedule Transform Your Life*' I place heavy emphasis on how to set a schedule to Fast. It works, but only if you work it. I suggest using that schedule to help you with the process of letting God's Spirit help you get strong enough to ignore temptation in order to prevent fornication. A very significant way that I treat temptation, is by liking it to POISON. For example, there are certain things I just will not put in my body because they are poisonous. Such as cigarettes, drugs, alcohol, and many others.

Treat temptation and fornication this way, essentially adding them to the list of poisons and toxic things that can kill you, you'll avoid them like the plague they are. Combine this with Fasting the first three days of every month and you're well on your way to victory!

THE SUCCESS

The success of overcoming fornication and the numerous temptations that comes with it, pays for itself in a happy home, happy marriage, happy wife, happy life.

Given that the devil is intent upon tearing down any happiness you've built up, by replacing them with strongholds in your life that he has control over, it is imperative that you learn to walk in the success of overcoming temptation 'before' it leads to fornication.

I've learned to look at fornication this way. If you submit to it, you're not only sleeping with that person, but you're attaching yourself to everyone they've ever slept with, and those spiritual ties come with some seriously crazy baggage.

Once you know this and learn to live like it, your success will begin to be measured by avoiding and having victory over the many forms of temptation that will come your way once you make the decision to live for God, rather than preparing to die with the devil.

There truly is no comparison.

HAVE YOU OVERCOME EXTRAORDINARY CIRCUMSTANCES & PUSHED PAST ROADBLOCKS & OBSTACLES IN YOUR LIFE?

Greetings,
I'm Pastor Keith...

I would be most grateful if you would share your story with my readers.

Visit my site and click 'Share Your Story'

SuccessAfterSetback.com

Success
After
Setback

Chapter
Two

THE SETBACK
~LIMITLESS LIES~

Lying is the language of the devil [John 8:42-44]. In my early teens and into adulthood I was out of control because I used lying as a way to survive. I used it to eat and to keep a roof over my head. I didn't just start lying one day. I was taught by one of my brothers. He would take me to work with him where he delivered beverages to homes and businesses on a truck. As the young impressionable mind I was at the time, I listened and soaked up his every mannerism and every word. His approach was told to me in detail most times. He would tell me who he was going to target and how he was going to do it, and what he was going to get from them. It worked every time. He has a natural gift of gab and people believed him. They would give him exactly what he said he would ask for. I knew what he was telling them was lies. I did not know how dangerous it was.

In 1980 when my dad passed away, I was 17. I was unable to support myself. My siblings and I received money from the various insurance policies and annuities that my dad set up for his retirement. I ran through the check within a week. I purchased stereo equipment; gave away money; and bought lots of marijuana. My brother Buck, a Vietnam Veteran, stepped in to take over our family home. He worked for the city as a bus driver and could afford the $126 monthly mortgage payment and the additional funds necessary to keep up with the other bills such as utilities.

There was one problem: Buck was a drug addict. Vietnam damaged him. His keeping up the payments did not last long. Months went by. I remember a phone call from a lawyer who asked me if I had $1,066 to pay off the tax bill for the house before it would foreclose. For me, the call came a week too late. I had the money the week before. I'm sure my siblings received the same phone call, but none of them responded to help save our home. The foreclosure went through and the house was lost. At the time, it was worth $45,000. My mom and dad worked hard to get that home so it would always be in the family. Because my siblings were too selfishly living their own lives by that point, and didn't want the burden of taking care of their troubled and rebellious little brother, they left me to fend for myself.

After the house was taken and I had to move. I couldn't live with any of my other siblings. I was too troubled and rebellious over losing both my mom and my dad, and being molested the night my mom died. Lying became second nature to me because it was a matter of survival. I had never been taught how to fend for myself, so I used the one thing I was taught to get money and it worked. My lies became limitless. People either believed me or they didn't care. They gave me what I asked for. That part of my life was the greatest setback of all. I never knew that lying, like your fingerprint, identifies you and often can define you. Like a fingerprint, it's nearly impossible to remove. To this day, my brother, in his 70s, is still lying. I chose to stop, but the devil did not give up easily.

THE CHALLENGE

The challenge to stop lying was much more difficult that I thought it would be. I believed that I could just stop because I knew it was wrong. We are made of flesh. Once our flesh gets a hold of something that goes against God, the devil steps in to help make sure your flesh stays weak. It makes it that much more difficult to break whatever stronghold has taken root in your life.

The challenge to stop lying was difficult because telling the truth exposes, uncovers, unveils and often points out flaws within us that we typically don't want anyone else to see. The very thing I didn't want others to see was exactly what I needed help with.

I needed people to know that I was hurting, grieving, feeling abandoned, rebelling and acting out because my mom and my dad were gone and I didn't know why!

Lying became a shield for me to keep people from knowing the truth about my messed up life.

My life had gone from being in a happy family with church and dinner table Sundays to my mom dying, and then my dad, and my siblings all scattering leaving me alone to fend for myself. I was 17 on the south side of Chicago where gangs and drugs were rampant. I was utterly, completely, and totally devastated and I used lying as a way to keep people from knowing it.

THE PROCESS

The process of overcoming the stronghold of falsehood, lying, deception and anything related, starts with facing the truth about yourself, your life, and its reality. The process is quite simple yet quite difficult if you don't follow the course already charted for all of us. That course is crystal clear and it's detailed and summarized in one scripture: *"The truth shall set you free."*

Adopting this 'set free' model works. It works because it has to. It's God's Word. It's living and breathing, designed to do exactly what God says it will do. When God says it will set you free, He means it. It sets us free from lying; every circumstance surrounding that lie; and every person whose lives the lies affect. Lying has consequences as well as accountability. Once we tell the truth another scripture steps in and helps the one that sets us free. That scripture is *"All things work together for the good of those who love God and are the called according to His purpose."* Lying stopped for me about 95% the day I started being accountable to God, to myself, to my wife and to my kids. Accountability in business relationships came later. I was supremely proud of reaching 95% because it began to help me to see that there was another way and that way is called the truth. People appreciate the truth because they can rely on it. They come to know you as honest and reliable and dependable and forthright. Not much is greater than that. A good name is better than silver and gold, and that too, is scripture. Whatever your process is to overcome telling lies, start now. You'll be glad where you finish.

THE SUCCESS

The success of overcoming lying has numerous benefits, all of which are good for you, and for those around you. Just like lying affects everything and everyone around you, the truth affects everything and everyone around you as well. The difference between the truth and a lie is that the truth is going to open doors that bring delight into your life whereas lying brings nothing but darkness.

Honesty and integrity are other fantastic benefits of telling the truth. Maturity comes along with that because it's very grown up to speak the truth. Truth has elements attached to it that only surface and benefit you when you tell the truth. It is our moral compass.

In addition, the truth has protections that go along with it that are there to help and aide in your defense, when you use the truth as a weapon against any lie. These defenses help protect you from all sorts of backlash that the devil can bring your way IF you're not prayed up and girded by a belt of truth that prevents him from penetrating your protective covering called the truth.

The truth is the only thing that can set us free. The more you use it the better off you'll always be. The devil is afraid of you telling the truth because lying is his native language and there is no truth in him. When you tell the truth, you are speaking a foreign language to him that he cannot understand. And he cannot attack something that he cannot understand.

THE SETBACK
~NEGATIVE OUTCOMES~

I began experiencing negative outcomes at a very early age. At the time, I didn't know it had anything to do with the calling God has on my life, but it became evident the more it happened. When these experiences would occur, it would be a totally opposite outcome from any other person who had just gone through the same experience. Their outcome would be positive; mine would always be negative.

This setback has been and still is
'a continual and daily battle' in my life

My first negative outcome was when my sister Renee came home from having surgery for what I was told was treatment for Tuberculosis. She was in a wheelchair. I was five years old. I was angry that she had taken over my play space in the basement. I remember she said something to the effect that I should go play somewhere else. I slapped her square in the face. That was 45 years ago. My sister has only spoken to me or seen me less than a dozen times since then. The negative outcome is that my actions caused me to lose the close relationship that my sister and I once had.

The second negative outcome I remember was four years later. My mom had passed away and I was angry because of the lack of communication around her death.

No one ever said a word about my mom after the funeral. When I was age nine, my sister Kim had a small bronze chest where she kept certain valuables under lock and key. It sat on her dresser. I was told to leave it alone. I didn't. I found the key, opened it, and took a single silver dime that she was saving because she knew it would be valuable some day. I took it to the corner store and bought candy with it. She eventually forgave me, but things were never the same. It was the very first time I had stolen anything. The negative outcome is that it laid the foundation for many years of taking things. A few years later I took her new, white, 10-speed Schwinn bicycle for a ride to Ogden Park in spite of my dad telling me not to. The bike got stolen. She hadn't even had the chance to ride it yet.

Negative outcomes can be changed, altered, and avoided altogether using one simple Biblical rule: *"Do unto others as you would have them do unto you."*

You can't expect different outcomes
if you keep repeating the same actions

Learning these two things has helped me tremendously since discovering that my outcomes were different than anyone else who had the same experiences.

If you don't learn from a negative outcome
you are most likely to repeat it.

THE CHALLENGE

The challenge to prevent and altogether avoid negative outcomes has been with me most of my life. I have done and still do everything I can to prevent and avoid such occurrences. I have yet to master or even figure out a formula that works other than avoiding relationships with people completely, which is impossible.

I've learned throughout this process that no matter what I've done or tried to do over the past 45 years of my life I'm the one who usually gets blamed, targeted, called to the carpet, and a host of other outcomes. I keep moving forward in spite of the negative outcomes designed to keep me off track and distracted on the path to my calling and living out my destiny.

THE PROCESS

Negative outcomes in my life is a stronghold designed and purposed to keeping me from completely overcoming all adverse conditions, relationships, associations and occurrences that stand in the way of my destiny. This stronghold latched on my willingness to walk into the calling on my life and does everything it can from keeping me from moving forward. Look at it this way. 50% of the people I get involved with in any relationship, situation or circumstance ends up positive, and 50% end up negative. Some would say those are fairly standard and average odds but I can assure you that for a man of God, called to be a pastor, teacher and shepherd over God's people those odds are very lopsided and dangerous. Such outcomes can only serve to prevent people from trusting in your leadership.

I do experience the 50 positive outcomes out of 100. It's not enough for me. Typically for a man in my position of leadership it should be around 98% or better, consistently.

The process of getting rid of negative outcomes in your life will most likely be different for you than it is for me. If your negative outcomes are precipitated by your own doing, it will require you to change your attitude, your focus, and your actions. However, if some of the negative outcomes are perpetrated by others, you will need to learn how to ignore their actions, pray your way through it, pray for them along the way, and focus on a new path. Once you're forging a new path, you will spend less time focused on anyone or anything that may be doing or intends to do you harm.

I focus my prayers on Isaiah 54:17; Psalm 37:4; Mathew 5:44. These scriptures help me to keep my focus 'off' my enemy and 'on' my task at hand. For example, after getting out of jail after a six month stint once, while on probation I focused all my efforts on programming the best software I could for a client. It earned me $45/hr. Plenty of reason not to focus on anything but the project. Another example while on probation is that instead of letting my mind think about being under surveillance, I wrote and published many books, built a bookstore/cafe` and a tea and beverage brand.

Nothing should stop you from the process
of overcoming negative outcomes in your life.

THE SUCCESS

The success of overcoming negative outcomes in your life presents a number of benefits that will be evident over periods of time after each and every individual circumstance. For example, you won't know the outcome to a relationship you're in until it ends. Or, you won't know the outcome of a project you're working on until it's completed. Or, you won't be able to assess the outcome of a new business you've started until at least a year after the business has found its niche and customers have settled into you as a merchant.

Negative outcomes can be turned into positive ones, if:
1. You admit that there is a problem.
2. Identify what the problem is.
3. Work on the problem with a solution in mind.
4. Take the steps necessary to achieve the solution.

Focusing on taking the necessary steps to achieve the solution of a positive outcome is of utmost importance if you plan to have success in turning your negative outcomes into positive ones. You may never be able to go back and alter any past negative outcomes, but you can certainly work toward making positive ones going forward. Focus your efforts on doing that and you'll be just fine.

THE SETBACK
~FELONIES~

I've witnessed felonies destroy the hopes, dreams and aspirations of many. As a black man, I've seen a great disparity in how men in my culture are treated with the stigma of a felony record, over men in other cultures.

I have several felonies. Each has set me back in some way. I've learned how to move beyond them. Others constantly try to keep me burdened under the stigma. I've learned to use them as motivation, a springboard, and reminders of how to turn these setbacks into successes.

Every felony, no matter what type it is or what crime it is can cause setbacks. It can disrupt your life if you have to go to jail for punishment and to correct the behavior that precipitated the felony. It can cause major damage to your reputation. It can cause stress, strain and difficulty within your family, and a host of other resulting setbacks, such as loss of income to help support your family while you are serving time.

I know people whose entire families have alienated them because of their felony. I know others who have lost parental rights, had spouses divorce them while they were incarcerated, and many things that can be considered setbacks.

THE CHALLENGE

Working to overcome felonies in my life presented a unique challenge. I had to get past the initial shock and reality that when applying for jobs, whenever I was fortunate enough to get an interview, my felonies would be the focus of most of it. My skills are such that I've generally been able to earn six figures in most positions I've had. Whether it was designing software or designing buildings, I'm qualified to do that and more. However, as a black man, no level of skill can typically stand up against a felony.

I said '*typically*'. I'm not the type of person to let anyone using my felonies against me stand in the way of my progress. After all, this book is titled "*Success After Setback*" and I mean just that. To overcome the challenge of people looking at you as if you're nothing but a felon, you must first realize that **you're much more than a felon**. Some lyrics within one of my favorite songs are:

+ **You are more than the choices that you've made**
+ **You are more than the sum of your past mistakes**
+ **You are more than the problems you create**
+ **You've been remade.**

This simple truth should propel you and carry you through each and every problem you create, and each and every single challenge you face as a felon. My challenge to you is to get up, get out there, & keep knocking on doors because eventually one of them will open.

THE PROCESS

The process of turning felony setbacks from your past into future successes takes prayer, patience, and persistence, because it pays. You have to be willing to ask God for exactly what you want. If that means expungement, pray for it. Then take the steps necessary to make it happen. Remember, it makes no sense to ask God for something, then step out on faith and 'do' what it takes to get it. God is moved by 'Faith', not by need. Everyone has needs, but not everyone has faith. If you use your felony as motivation for your faith, I believe God will move in your favor. If you're asking God for a job, pray, then prepare a resume. Not just any resume, a 'great' one! One that looks like you 'want' the job.

THE SUCCESS

The success of overcoming felonies can be measured in many ways including the doors that caring people open to you in spite of your conviction or criminal record. There will always be people who will not accept you because of your felony. Get over it and move on. Don't give any space or thought to people who judge your character because of something that happened in your past, even if it's recent past.

I highly encourage you to get connected with nonprofits and other groups that assist with and help former felons reintegrate into society through job groups, referrals, training programs, and actual hiring because networking is a major key to success, especially as a felon.

Other ways you can overcome felonies include:

+ **Public speaking**

  o Telling your story can be therapeutic and helpful to others.

+ **Ministering to prisoners**

  o Who better to do this than someone who's been through it?

+ **Becoming an Advocate**

  o Your passion for turning your life around can launch a career.

+ **Help other former felons find jobs**

  o After one of my brief periods of incarceration I wrote a book titled, *"Build Your Resume The Right Way"* to teach others how to make their resumes stand out above all others, especially when you have a felony.

+ **Volunteer at places where other felons are**

  o Networking is a major key to the success of finding a job when you're a felon. Other felons may know where to find work.

+ **Ask for help**

  o Keep knocking on doors. Keep asking for help. Keep showing people that you want help. Participate in support groups where help exists. Get involved with Job Clubs where typically tons of resources and referrals exist.

THE SETBACK
~VICTIMS~

When you've committed a crime, although it isn't always against individuals, people are affected in some way. In my own situation, I had a real estate business that needed capital to operate. I borrowed money from investors to undertake several rehab projects.

An opportunity presented itself to earn a contract for a large development project. In order to participate I had to set aside the rehab projects. I made the decision to pursue the development project. Although it was approved by the neighborhood association, I made a bad decision.

The money I borrowed was secured against properties I had purchased on contract. When investors called their loans earlier than anticipated, claiming breach of contract because I pursued the development and I couldn't repay them all at once, I was put in jail.

The investors became victims, I became a felon, and from then on I was treated as if I swindled people out of money, rather than the truth of making a bad business decision. Not focusing all my efforts on the rehab projects rather than the development was a bad decision. One lesson I learned is that although the development project meant potential millions, keeping my word and doing one rehab at a time was the right, honorable and contractual way.

THE CHALLENGE

Working to overcome the stigma of being perceived as a swindler, and paying investors back their money plus interest, is a major challenge but not an impossible one.

In spite of being shown the potential millions in income in the development project, investors typically don't see eye to eye with your company goals when their money is involved in another portion of your business. Again, I got sidetracked and made a bad decision.

They invested in rehab, not potential or speculative or even approved development. They expected me to focus all my attention in that area, so they could be paid from the rehab profits. They were right.

I made a bad business decision and it cost me my reputation, trustworthiness, the investors, the development, ability to approach anyone else about any other project in the future, and my freedom.

Overcoming this challenge took facing it head on. I needed to take the steps necessary to restore what I had borrowed, even if that meant it would take me years to do so. Even though there was the additional difficulty of being a felon added to the already tough situation, it still isn't impossible to overcome.

In such a challenge, your biggest hurdle is finding or creating a way to earn enough to pay people back their money. Period.

THE PROCESS

Even when there's no intent to commit a crime, once you've been charged, convicted, and sentenced, the people you hurt are called victims. The process of overcoming this setback takes hard work and it will not be easy. Losing someone's trust means you may never get it back. When things break down in any relationship even a business one it can ruin you if you let it. The process of climbing back up from the low place you may sink to behind the stigma that you've hurt people in some way starts one dollar at a time if it's financial; one step at a time if it's relational. You should be prepared to face the reality that the relationship between you and whoever it is you hurt may never be repaired. You may have to move forward knowing people think you're just a felon who can't change.

THE SUCCESS

The success of overcoming a setback that leaves victims or angry people in its wake takes prayer that they will forgive you; patience while they are going through the healing process; and persistence to not give up. Success will be determined by what 'you' do going forward. Focus on moving ahead with your life; getting a new job or starting a new career; launching a new business; rebuilding your reputation; staying honest; maintaining your integrity; being dependable and reliable; etc. Doing these things, you will pay less attention and spend less energy on relationships from your past that you cannot mend.

THE SETBACK
~ENEMIES~

What is an enemy?

How can your enemy set you back?

How can you turn that into success?

Enemies can come in many shapes, forms, sizes, classes, cultures, and economic status. Enemies can be made on any day at any time behind any reason. For example, many people don't like me because I'm black. Others who don't like me because I've been with the same woman for over 29 years. Some who can't stand me because I don't hide my faith. Those who don't like me because of how gifted, skilled, and talented God made me. There are even people who don't like me because of various projects I've completed in spite of the myriad of hurdles I've faced and obstacles they've put in my way.

Admittedly, I've done things and made some decisions that created an atmosphere for people to dislike what I've done, or not like decisions I've made. There have been instances and situations that were entirely my fault, and many that weren't.

Whatever woodwork and rocks your enemies rise up from you should always remember that this is only a setback and that '*this too shall pass*'. Let me teach you how to overcome your enemies even if you created them.

THE CHALLENGE

The challenge to overcome and stay steps ahead of your enemies starts with you being able to deal with them without letting your emotions get the best of you. Many situations can run your blood-pressure through the roof, and skyrocket your anger to levels that may take a cold shower or counting way pass ten to calm. Enemies can do some hateful and vindictive things. They can be difficult to deal with if you're not emotionally strong enough to brace for the initial impact and the thoughts that will naturally run through your mind. If you can cushion yourself for an attack and deal with their attitude and your feelings of wanting to retaliate when you learn of it, you'll be just fine. Resilience is key.

The challenge is **not to**:
+ Act or react irrationally
+ Respond or reply too quickly
+ Let your emotions get the best of you.

Instead, be calm, rational and let your peaceful self do the talking rather than an overly excited and emotional one. Or, you can and will escalate the situation to levels higher than originally meant, anticipated, or necessary. Once an enemy becomes sworn to hurt you there's not much you can do about their actions. What counts is how you react and respond to it. Done right, you can often diffuse and de-escalate a situation just by how you react and respond to it. The initial shock is often the worst, and if you can get through that the rest can be quite simple.

THE PROCESS

The process of overcoming the setback of enemies starts with you recognizing who your real enemy is. First and foremost, the devil is your biggest enemy. No amount or level of activity or harm coming from any human or group of humans, could ever measure up to the variety and intensity of schemes the devil can throw at you.

There are many ways to begin the process of overcoming enemies and many pathways to get there. I highly recommend staring with the easiest, which is prayer. Praying for your enemy adds God's power to the equation. With God's power on your side, all you need to have the faith that it can work then put your faith into action by taking the steps necessary to move the mountain called 'your enemy' out of your path, off your case, and out of your life.

Prayer changes things. Answers to prayer are only activated by our faith. Most people think that God meets our needs from our prayer. Not true. God is moved by faith. Everyone has needs. God is moved by faith that is coupled with works (action) to take the steps necessary to move in your situation of need.

I highly recommend you get my latest CD, titled:

A Pastor's Prayer

It contains some of my most heartfelt prayers and petitions to God during some of the toughest times. It includes prayers for many people, situations and circumstances.

God says:

- + He supplies all our needs according to His riches in glory.
- + He also says that faith without works is dead.
- + He also says what good is it to see someone in need if you just pray for them without taking the steps to meet their needs?

Enemies that attack you, bring chaos, or wreak havoc in your life can be defeated through prayer, patience, and persistence. However, the most important ingredient is 'love'. Loving your enemy can be difficult when you see or know that someone has intent to harm you. Love is vital to your growth, necessary for your healing, and essential for you forgiving them, them forgiving you, and God forgiving both of you.

THE SUCCESS

Being successful over setbacks from enemies means that you've withstood whatever attack or onslaught they sent your way. And hopefully you've recognized or discovered whatever made you their enemy in the first place so that if it's something within your own behavior that you need to change you can do so.

Ultimately, the greatest level of success you'll achieve over enemies is no longer having them as an enemy. Remember, your biggest and most persistent enemy is the devil. He wants to do everything possible to keep you distracted with a deluge of destruction placed in your day. Keep the faith, stay focused, and move forward knowing he has already been defeated and Revelation 20:10 seals his fate.

Success After Setback

Chapter Three

THE SETBACK
~FORECLOSURE~

I experienced my first foreclosure before I even knew what it was. It was 1980. I was 17 years old. My mom had passed 8 years earlier and my dad had just passed six month ago. I was in the house they left behind with my drug addicted brother. My other siblings had already moved on. There were taxes to pay: just over a thousand dollars. As siblings we had the money, individually, and collectively.

No one in my family responded to the repeated phone calls from the attorney who had settled my Dad's estate, which left all of us a sizeable amount of money, but didn't allocate funds to pay the taxes on the house after he died. Because no one responded, six months after my Dad passed away the house was taken, for $1,066 in taxes. The home my mom and dad worked hard to get and keep for our family, gone.

I list this as a setback in my life because shortly after the house was taken I ended up homeless a few years. I slept on park benches and at the Pacific Garden Mission when they had beds available. I was working for Continental Bank in Remittance banking and Marshall Fields toy department, but I had no place to call home. Things changed when I worked for a company for a year whose employees stayed in hotels while we traveled. When my wife and I met in 1984 we lived with her mom until I got a place of my own in 1986.

The worst cases of foreclosure I've ever witnessed in this country occurred in 2008 when the truth began to surface about the greed in the banking, mortgage, and related industries. This crisis affected tens of millions of people and caused many of them to lose their homes, and end up homeless. My wife and I lost one of the homes caught up in the banking and mortgage scandal. A simple rambler at 8318 5th Ave in Bloomington, MN to some, but to us, is was home.

THE CHALLENGE

The challenge to overcome the setback of foreclosure is different for everyone. My situation happened because both my parents passed away and no one in my family cared enough to pay off the $1,066 to take care of the tax debt to save the home. My parents worked hard and paid for that home. To lose it like that was a travesty. The foreclosure affected me because and as a young man, 17 years old on the south side of Chicago, it was difficult to cope. The challenge for me was to find a place of my own. Impossible in the state of mind I was in because I cared more about buying Marijuana to mask my pain, than saving money from my inheritance or my paychecks. That eventually changed and I learned what other homeless people who wanted to live somewhere did in that situation. I rented a room and began the journey of being an adult. I met homelessness head on. I knew I wasn't supposed to be on the streets. I knew I had gifts, skills, talents, and abilities that were useful to somebody somewhere. I knew that all I had to do was apply myself and eventually doors would open up, and they did.

THE PROCESS

The process of overcoming foreclosure can take many turns, but the most important aspect is that once you're on the course that's right for your situation, you must stick to it.

Defeating foreclosure will take time. (1) There are documents you'll need such as copies of your mortgage(s); (2) There will be sacrifices you may have to make by forgoing paying for those extracurricular activities you're used to so that you can afford a good legal eagle, unless you plan to do it yourself. But if you're not planning to fight the foreclosure, then forget the first two items and the next two and go straight to the next paragraph. (3) You will need strength through prayer because you are fighting against greed. (4) You may lose the equity in your property and may have to walk away from it.

If you're not planning to fight against the foreclosure then let's talk about you moving forward. There's a great song to use for motivation. It's an unplugged version by Israel Houghton titled *Moving Forward*. He is on stage with another guitar player and a pianist. It's online. I used this song to get me through losing assets built over several years and this version is by far my favorite. Moving forward after foreclosure means letting go of the past. It will take cherishing the moments you were blessed with during the time you had the property, treasuring those for what they are, and letting them go. You can hold on to mementos, but by all means, let go of any bad memories, learn from them and move on.

To walk into newness you must first walk out of what is dead and gone. You can do it. It may take time to get enough strength to let go of the past, but once you do, you will be able to take hold of the new thing that God has for you, and new places He can give you.

THE SUCCESS

Again, my wife and I experienced one foreclosure. In business, I've had dozens from many properties I owned through 2008. Success after foreclosure doesn't mean that you will get another property. It could be as simple as letting go of the old one. In one of my foreclosure situations, I spiritually felt that God would not Bless me with a new home until I was fully out of the old one.

By saying 'fully' I mean not hanging on to old furniture, keeping things in storage from your old house that are hindering your growth, and so on.

Once I let go of the old, dead things, God gave me new things. Letting go of the old one made room for what God had in store for me.

Here's a little testimony: *"The new house has made me forget many things about the old one, but God has let me remember where He brought me from!"*

So, walk into the future by letting go of the past!

THE SETBACK
~LAWSUITS~

I've had a few failed businesses, which were temporary setbacks. I say temporary because the myriad of things I learned in the process of failure, motivated me straight into future successes.

I never let the setback of a failed business stop me. I used it to encourage me into these words: *"The Lord Will Make a Way Somehow"* and *"If at First You Don't Succeed, Try Again"*.

Trying again is what helped me succeed every time. Failure is a great motivator for success. Don't get me wrong, I did a number of things along the way that helped me get back up, dust off, grab hold of my bootstraps and keep moving, one step and one day at a time.

Those things included reading motivational books such as:
+ *The Power of Positive Thinking*
+ *Rich Dad Poor Dad*
+ *Who Moved My Cheese*

...and many others. And, I watched all the TD Jakes videos I could find, but I never let any failure send me into a place of fear or depression. Had I allowed myself to sink into either of these places, I would not have been in a state of mind that helped me understand and deal with the variety and number of lawsuits that often come as a result of a failed business.

Lawsuits can be a matter of course. Sometimes it's personal, sometimes not. I had to learn that. What kept me moving forward was knowing that *'This too shall pass'*. In order to get beyond the negative feelings that can come with lawsuits, I focused on making progress and being successful in the next project so that I could generate income to pay off what I failed at in the past and the resulting lawsuits. Lawsuits can set you back emotionally, financially, physically, and spiritually, especially when other Christians sue you. Lawsuits can damage your reputation and be a hurdle for anyone who would consider helping you in your next venture.

THE CHALLENGE

The challenge to overcome lawsuits behind a failed business takes prayer. I prayed for patience because it took a lot of it. And I needed more than my own strength to help get me through them, because some of the fallout in my situations ended up being broadcast on television and the newspapers articles. Lawsuits are a challenge in any situation. When someone sues you they typically expect to win. Because they expect to win they also anticipate receiving something from you. However, there are laws in place that can protect you and your business from the often overwhelming feeling of dread that can come with being sued. One of the laws in place is called "Bankruptcy". Over 15 years, I had to file a handful of times. I'm not alone. Many well known entrepreneurs have done the same thing. I highly suggest researching this and other laws that can protect and help you through lawsuits.

THE PROCESS

The process of getting past the setback that lawsuits can bring takes much work. Lawsuits can place hurdles in front of any new venture you've started and lessen your credibility. There's not much worse than having a new venture that's showing profitably and success and being served papers saying you're being sued from an old venture. But something else I learned helped me get through this kind of difficulty and setback as well. It's called 'Things Happen'.

Given that you typically have no control over how, when, or at what level things happen, you should learn to take it on the chin and keep your feet moving forward taking it all in stride.

This comfort and confidence did not come overnight. It took a few of these situations before I became seasoned in the process as well as learning to pray my way through them. I had to ignore the fact that lawsuits are public information. I had to get over the fact that depending on who you are a lawsuit could bring the media to your door.

I had to understand that a lawsuit could cause harm to any reputation I had left. I had to get through the lawsuits by hiring a lawyer when I could afford them and even when I couldn't. And when I couldn't, I either allowed the lawsuits to default for whoever was suing me, threw myself on the mercy of the court, or asked the person suing me for more time to get things in order.

Doing damage control around lawsuits is often as simple as hiring a public relations expert who has experience in dealing with your type of situation. It's important to respond to any lawsuit because if you don't, the public or the court never has opportunity to hear your side of the story. And your side of the story could be anything under the sun as long as it's the truth. Hardship may not stop a lawsuit but the reason behind the hardship could be compelling enough to have whoever sued you, to have compassion on you enough to back off until you can get back on your feet and start making things right. I've had lawsuits go in any number of directions but the one common denominator overall is that the truth is what set me free.

THE SUCCESS

Success after lawsuits may have nothing to do with getting past the lawsuit itself. It may be as simple as having the courage to stand your ground through the process, or as complex as putting together a strategy and hiring an attorney to defend your rights. It may have nothing to do with winning, but rather may be as easy as knowing you told your side of the story so that there wouldn't just be a one-sided opinion of what happened.

Success after lawsuits can elevate to a level wherein you have paid off any resulting damages to the other party, or entered into an agreement that you can comfortably manage and afford.

The point is, 'to do something', that's the success.

THE SETBACK
~JUDGMENTS & LIENS~

Lawsuits often result in judgments against you. Judgments from lawsuits are often monetary with timelines involved. These can be financial setbacks. And, they can add blips to your personal and business credit report.

Judgments can come without lawsuits. These typically come from you owing taxes to either the state or federal government. In addition to the judgment they can place a lien on anything of value you own, place the debt in first position on any mortgage, and capture funds from your bank account and tax refunds, often without your permission, or knowledge.

Liens can also be setbacks. They can come without lawsuits. Liens can be filed because you haven't paid a contractor for work they performed for you. These can also be difficult because they are typically public information.

There are many other forms of judgments and liens and the outcome of them all depend on what the situation is, and the outcome sought by the person or company seeking money from you.

As with lawsuits, the most important thing to do in these situations is to respond, try to work them out, and get the creditor(s) paid.

THE CHALLENGE

The challenge to overcome judgments and liens takes work. I like to say it like this: '*You can overcome debt one dollar at a time.*' Once you've paid off a judgment you typically will receive a Release of Judgment. When you've paid off a lien you generally receive a Lien Release. This doesn't automatically get rid of any notices on your personal or business credit report. It can take multiple letters, copies of the ... or lien release, and then they may only drop off of your file when the reporting agencies are tired of you writing or calling them. The challenge, if you're willing to accept it, can be lengthy, time consuming, frustrating at times, and you may feel like giving up, but you have to find strength through prayer, be patient and persistent, and it will eventually pay off.

THE PROCESS

The process of getting past the setback of judgments and liens is not much different than what you need to do to get past lawsuits. There are some things that you can do to help speed the process of paying off and removing judgments and liens. For example:

+ Set up a payment agreement 'before' a lawsuit is ever filed.

+ Set up a payment agreement 'before' a lien is ever filed.

+ Make a sacrifice to give up a nonessential item (such as smoking).

+ Take the money from smoking and use it to pay judgments/liens.

+ Make it your mission to pay judgments/liens.

These are just a few of the essentials that I suggest and recommend you start with.

THE SUCCESS

Success after judgments and liens will come in the form of more paperwork. Release of Judgment and Lien Releases are typically what you'll receive once the payments have been made.

Sacrifice will bring success in these situations, and your prayer, patience and persistence will eventually pay off.

THE SETBACK
~BANKRUPTCY~

Bankruptcy is a financial setback but it's also an opportunity to start fresh and get it right. I've been through bankruptcy a handful of times because I thought it was the only way to stop the constant harassing phone calls. Other emotionally draining processes and issues come along with being in debt. Bankruptcy to me, was a sign of failure. Although it gave me the ability to start over, in retrospect, I wouldn't go that route again. Working through debt without bankruptcy is much more fulfilling, responsible, and let's your creditors know that you're willing to stand up and take responsibility for what you owe and work a plan to get it paid.

THE CHALLENGE

I no longer know all the nuances nor have I kept up with the pros and cons of filing bankruptcy because it's been over 15 years since I needed to file. There are some definite benefits to using the protection, but also note that there are some major setbacks that you will experience as a result. The challenge to overcome bankruptcy starts with the commitment to stay out of debt. That is often difficult because of the credit based society that we live in. Once you can show that you have the ability to pay, companies will issue you credit cards at will. If you're not strong enough to say, "No, I don't need to take out a loan and/or pay interest, just to buy a shirt or blouse," you are well on your way to overcoming bankruptcy.

74

THE PROCESS

Bankruptcy didn't eliminate all of my debt but it did get rid of most of it. The fallout of having bankruptcy on your credit report can only be overcome by: (1) Opening new credit accounts (2) Showing a consistent track record of paying bills (3) Keeping a steady income stream (4) Establishing a savings plan and sticking to it.

None of this will happen overnight. It will take time. Prayer, patience, and persistence is key because some companies will not extend credit because you're in bankruptcy. These things and more are needed to recover from bankruptcy and another item is a budget. Budgeting is essential to the process of overcoming bankruptcy because you will need to control your spending and you'll need to be aware of your income and where you should be saving as well. Debt consolidation agencies may help before and after bankruptcy, but a good financial planner is worth their weight in gold.

Debit cards instead of credit cards keeps your spending intact because you can only spend what you have. Coming out of bankruptcy and starting fresh by getting new credit accounts established with a secured card, is beneficial, and helpful. Once you've spent about a year keeping that line of credit above par, there will most likely be opportunities to increase your credit limit. You can transition from the debit card to standard credit card, but I highly suggest you wait before jumping into that frying pan because it can often lead you right back into the same situation you just overcame.

THE SETBACK ◤   ▦THE CHALLENGE

THE SUCCESS

The success of overcoming bankruptcy starts with the quietness that will come almost immediately once you've filed and creditors are informed that you've done so. That quietness can bring peace of mind, help you sleep, relax, and rest, knowing that you've gotten through the worst of it and are headed toward a new beginning and a fresh start.

THE SETBACK
~DEBT~

Because of bad business decisions in my past, I've worked on paying off more than one million. Most of it consists of business debt accumulated over the past fifteen years; 10% personal debt; 5% taxes; 15% restitution.

Debt is a setback. The majority of my debt came when a handful of creditors, presumably led by a former employee of mine, saw to it that I spend time in jail, which I did, for six months.

Another chunk of the business debt came from a high school I designed and built, combined with a real estate development company I owned before and while the bottom dropped out of the U.S. market.

I decided against bankruptcy for the real estate company and took the responsibility to work with investors and creditors and make the best of both a bad economic crisis, and my bad decisions. In some situations it worked. In others, it didn't.

I'm not one to let any setback keep me down. I held my head up, did my time, ministered to many people while incarcerated, served as the head cook for the warden, administrative and corrections staff, as well as 125 inmates, putting great, creative meals and spiritual guidance on the table three times a day.

THE CHALLENGE

The challenge to overcome being more than $1M in debt is generating enough income to make regular and sizeable payments to reduce the debt. And, to sacrifice anything that you may want or think you need in order to use the money to pay down the debt.

I've been a software programmer since the early 1980's. Since 1987 I've been able to make upwards of $50/hr *'when my eyes would let me work for long periods of time writing code'*. This is income, usable to pay down debt.

I'm also the author of numerous books. I'm able to produce income from book sales. I'm the owner of bookstore/cafes and a tea and beverage brand. I've worked hard to put myself in a position to be able to eliminate the balance of the entire debt within a few years, 'without bankruptcy" by being resilient and not giving up.

The challenge to overcoming what some see as a massive amount of debt is to be able to stay focused on making the payments. Don't get lackadaisical and lose zeal for paying it off. Stay focused. I didn't allow the debt to deter me from starting the next business. I built a publishing company; authored and released several books; and opened a retail store, while under the weight of debt. Some would say this is impossible, but I'm living proof that it can be done.

Put prayer, patience, and persistence to work. It eventually pays off.

THE PROCESS

The process of overcoming such a massive amount of debt without bankruptcy starts with being purposed to pay it off '**no matter how long it takes**'. This will drive you to doing the right thing, over the long term, and making it your mission to get it done.

Getting through and past such a large amount of debt will not be easy, but again, it can be done. But it's only going to work if you're willing to put every extra dollar that you have toward paying down the debt. Place the debt amount somewhere in your home where you can constantly see it such as the refrigerator. You will be reminded of it and motivated by it.

THE SUCCESS

The success of overcoming being more than $1M in debt is obviously getting out of debt. For me it was a little different than most people may think. My greatest motivator was to build the next venture, earn more income, and pay down more of the debt. Even if that means chipping away a little at a time.

I'm a visionary. I see progress in 3D. It's hard to explain but I can look at something and see the value in it before most ever catch up. It's where you get statements like: '*he's way ahead of his time.*' Or, '*he has a midas touch*'. It's nothing magical. It's a God-given gift that I don't take lightly or for granted.

Books & CD referenced on previous pages.

	From Page 18		From Page 36
Ten Years Ten Tears [My autobiography]		Transform Your Schedule Transform Your Life	
	From Page 54		From Page 59
Build Your Resume The Right Way		A Pastor's Prayer CD	

SuccessAfterSetback.com

HAVE YOU OVERCOME EXTRAORDINARY CIRCUMSTANCES & PUSHED PAST ROADBLOCKS & OBSTACLES IN YOUR LIFE?

Greetings,
I'm Pastor Keith...

I would be most grateful if you would share your story with my readers.

Visit my site and click 'Share Your Story'

SuccessAfterSetback.com

THE SETBACK   THE CHALLENGE

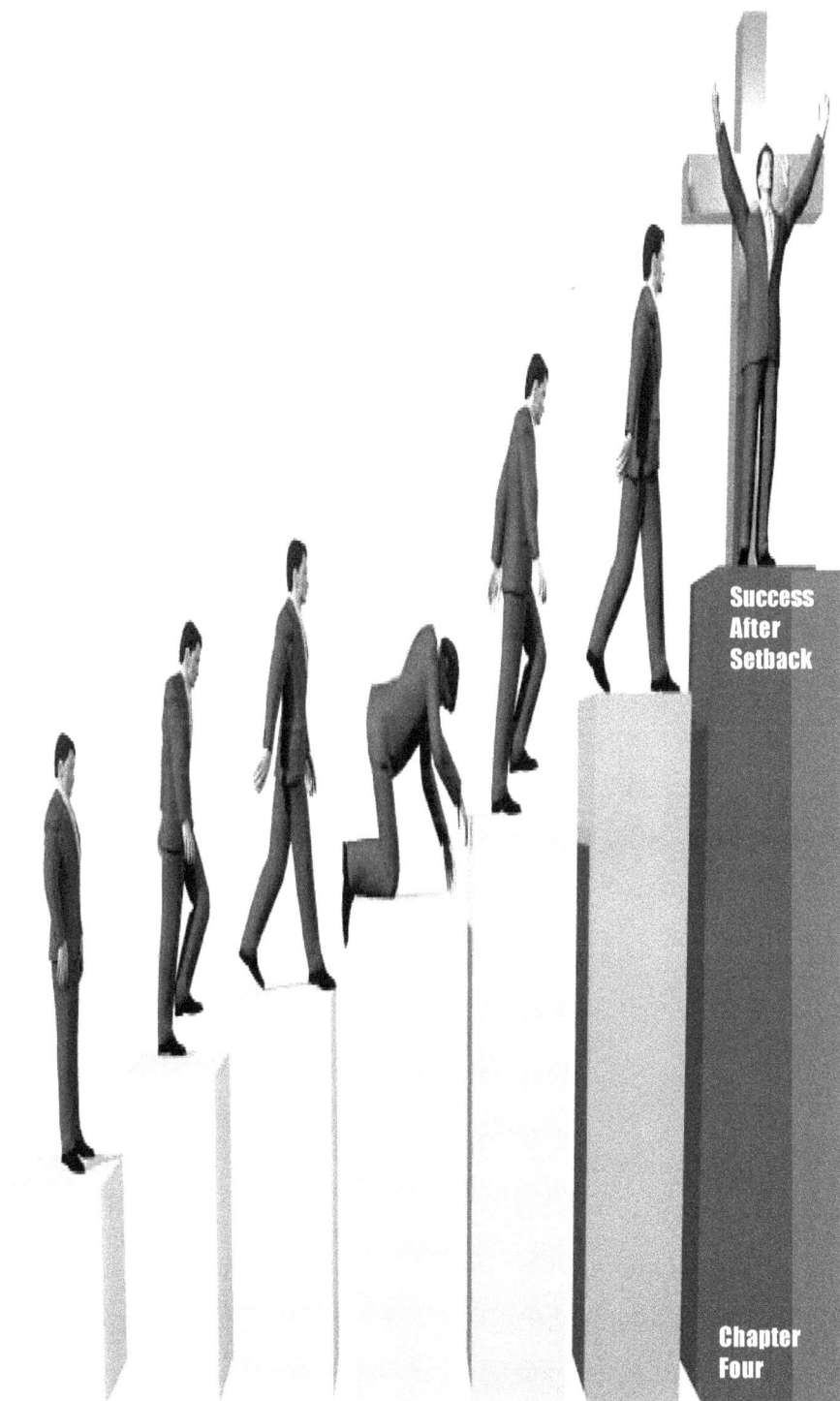

Success
After
Setback

Chapter
Four

THE SETBACK
~BURNED BRIDGES~

From as far back as I can remember in my early days in business I started burning bridges. I opened my first company in 1987 in Chicago as Hammond Construction. I got a business license; leased a small office in a high-rise downtown and hired a secretary. I took basic labor jobs sweeping up construction sites. Eventually I learned the RFP process and began bidding on larger projects. I placed an ad and accepted applications for laborers in case I won the bid. A pro football player whose team had won the super bowl just a year earlier applied for a position. I was both shocked and interested in his story and I soon learned that drugs had found their way into his life. He was broke and needed work. We didn't work together, but because he had several kids and the rambler he lived in had a mortgage, I helped him in a very small financial way, and was glad to do it. He's a pro coach today.

The setback came in the form of burning a bridge with the local unions. I had no idea that the Davis-Bacon Act even existed nor did I understand what prevailing wages were. I soon learned. I received a collective visit from three local union reps. They politely informed me that I could not bid on contracts in the city, if I wasn't intent upon hiring union workers and paying union scale. And, they told me that I could no longer accept any jobs as a labor contractor if I wasn't going to hire union labor to do the work.

I couldn't afford it. Before I knew it, my mouth muttered some-thing to the effect of them not telling me who I could and could not hire. They looked at each other, got up out of the chairs seated in front of my desk, and without a word, walked out of my office. Long story short, I was never able to bid on or even be awarded another job or contract in the city again. Burning that bridge taught me a very valuable lesson: Follow the rules.

I could write a book on the subject of burning bridges but this chapter is enough for now. I've burned many bridges in my decades of doing business. So many, that I cannot remember them all. Many were financial; some relational; others contractual. But the two things I learned throughout the process are: (1) each of them set me back in some way and (2) the outcomes didn't have to turn out that way.

THE CHALLENGE

The challenge to overcome a history of burning bridges in business took three things:

1. Willingness to ask others for assistance.
2. Delegating relationship building to those who know how.
3. Leaving the contract negotiations to the professionals.

In order to overcome the challenge I first had to meet it head on. This was not and has not been an easy task for me. All my life I've been used to doing things on my own; managing projects and processes on my own; dealing with the results and the fallout on my own. Throughout this process I learned that no man is an island.

84

THE PROCESS

The process of overcoming and getting past burning bridges in business and in life starts with:

+ Swallowing your pride.

+ Being honest and keeping your word.

+ Never cutting corners.

These are three basic things 'I' needed to learn before I was ever going to make any progress in this area. I had to swallow my pride in the area of thinking I already knew it all. I had to admit that I needed help. And, I had to be willing to listen. In the chapter "Building New Bridges" I explain much more about the benefits of being willing to do these three things, but for now, I'll focus on the benefits.

THE SUCCESS

The benefits of overcoming the setback of burning bridges in nearly every business relationship I've ever had are immeasurable. The first and most noticeable benefit is that with a team around you, it makes a world of difference because:

+ You're no longer the single POC for everything in the company.

+ You have buffers in place that shield you from operations.

+ You're free to focus on growing and marketing the company.

There is a seemingly endless list of benefits that come along with getting past the setback of burning bridges. Again, I spend more on this subject in the chapter on Building New Bridges, but I can tell you that letting go and delegating are by far the two most beneficial.

THE SETBACK
~BLACKLIST~

As a black man, I've felt like I've been blacklisted most of my life. At the age of 18 I began to notice how I wasn't treated the same as my white associates and co-workers. This came as a shock to me because in the community I grew up in until my Dad died I was sheltered and rarely saw or had any interaction with whites. The only thing I generally watched on TV was westerns, so I was oblivious to the prejudice that existed.

I mentioned in an earlier chapter that as a result of my first business, a construction company, where I told the local union reps that I intended to hire who I wanted, and not go broke trying to pay union scale, I never received another job or project after that. I was blacklisted.

The setback of being blacklisted has come in many forms, but it typically had the same effect. The same common denominator was true over each of my experiences, which is that I was pretty much at fault each and every time. Unless, however, someone was simply abusing their power or authority, which has also happened to me.

The union reps were my first experience with being blacklisted. That's no easy thing to overcome trying to build a business in a city as politically driven as Chicago.

I've had other experiences in other facets and areas of business over the years. The results are basically the same across the board: I was prohibited from having access to any resources that the people blacklisting me had control over, access to, or could connect with. Every door I tried to open, they contacted people who do to get them to blacklist me too. It's very difficult to overcome, but I fear no man and nothing is impossible for God.

THE CHALLENGE

The challenge to overcome being blacklisted starts with recognizing that it exists. Facing this stark reality is the only way to restore your good name, reputation, and make progress in your life. Forge a new pathway that is not related to the area(s) you've been blacklisted in, and work hard to make that path a success.

Here's an example: One of the areas I was blacklisted in was real estate. I was told both by some key players in the industry as well as the authorities who were in charge of the terms of my freedom that for the next 20 years I could not do any business in real estate, until and unless I paid off the money I owed as a result of my failed business. I saw the effects of this blacklist in ways too numerous to mention in the pages of this book.

Another example: I was also blacklisted from doing any computer programming because of my skills. At each job I applied for I would see people show up at the interview and secretly hand the receptionist my criminal history. Rather than complain I took it in stride and forged new paths instead of trying to get work in this area.

THE PROCESS

The process of overcoming the setback of being blacklisted is not easy. When there are people who have control over what you can and cannot do across entire cities, there isn't a process in the world that can help. What you have to do is (1) Trust God. (2) Be vigilant about forging a new path and faithful enough to walk down it.

Forging a new path may mean doing something as simple as getting a job at a fast food restaurant where the powers that be can see that you're at least making an effort to move forward, and willing to humble and humiliate yourself to get work.

It's not that simple for me. It's 2014. I'm 50 years old. I've never worked in fast food. Not because I wouldn't and I've certainly applied. I'm the type of person whereas if I'm going to work in a fast food restaurant, my sole purpose is going to be to learn the ins and outs so I can get on a fast track to owning that restaurant.

In my book titled: *"Do's and Dont's of Doing Business"* I point out that not following the rules is not a smart thing to do. Rules are in place to prevent chaos.

Whatever new path you forge, including a new business unrelated to the reason you've been blacklisted, put all your efforts, time and energy into it because prayer, patience and persistence will pay off. Again, trust God that it will.

THE SUCCESS

Overcoming the setback of being blacklisted has many benefits including getting out from under someone else's thumb. Another advantage is that if you don't focus on being blacklisted, instead putting your efforts into forging a new path, you're on your way to building income from a totally different and unrelated area.

This has tremendously positive implications that can be lifelong.

For example, in my past, while blacklisted, I designed, built and opened a high school. Most recently, while blacklisted, I built a publishing company, wrote and published several books, opened a bookstore/café', developed my own tea and beverage brand, and started generating income from these various 'new' streams.

NOTE: If you're thinking in the direction of wasting energy and resources to launch an investigation into who it is that blacklisted you, let me be the first to tell you it's not worth it. I found out who it was that kept me under their thumb, and given the tremendous evidence I gathered, I easily could have retaliated with lawsuits. But when God tells you to be still; leave room for his wrath; don't repay evil with evil; love and pray for your enemies, you have to believe that no weapon formed against you shall prosper. Many other scriptures speak to this situation.

My advice is to trust God and focus your time on your new path.

THE SETBACK
~SURVEILLANCE~

Have you ever seen a TV show where an actor playing a bad guy is being secretly watched by those in authority? This scenario may seem made for television, but it was part of my daily life for a few years.

In 1999, after working as a network admin and training inmates in data entry at the local women's prison and building a network for a nonprofit with four sites, I was approved for a $1M annual contract with a school district to design and build a new high school. Unheard of for any felon. Almost immediately, I began to notice people around me, looking at me, following me, talking into their sleeves. I thought I was crazy until I circled and doubled back around an aisle in a retail store, without this person noticing, and heard them giving a play-by-play of my activity in the store I was shopping in.

When I inquired of the powers that be I was told that it was because I had been quoted in some article that the school I was building wasn't going to be just another high school because I did not agree with the process of any school district green-stamping diplomas for kids who can't read. Needless to say, that statement stepped on a few toes at the top, and made me a few enemies. I built and opened the school, but it didn't last long. Because of that statement, and the fact that I was raising more funds that most and having more success with dropouts than the district, they cancelled my contract.

That wasn't my first experience dealing with being under surveillance. With my willingness to tell the truth publicly about certain issues, and express my opinions about topics others don't seem to want to address, it probably won't be the last. Maybe I'll try politics someday.

My most recent experience being under surveillance came with my release from jail in 2008. It's typical that certain types of former inmates get some level of administrative or intense supervision. From having to check in to parole or probation officers, to having an ankle bracelet; but 24-hour surveillance is something totally different.

Surveillance was a setback in my life but it also served to help bring another level of accountability. It helped me to realize that God has us under surveillance at all times. However, because He gives us free will and space to make mistakes, learn from them, and get back on track, I understood the process.

The closest thing I can use to describe what I've experienced is being on the other side of the movie 'Stakeout' where the major actors played the role as the authorities renting a house across from the home where a convict was suspected to eventually show up at. Ironically, watching that movie many years ago helped prepare me for these experiences. And, being in a gang where part of our regular activity was watching out for police trying to sneak into or infiltrate our block, heightened my senses beyond the norm for paying attention to detail and taking notice of people who are watching me.

THE CHALLENGE

The challenge to overcome the setback of being under surveillance is to first simply ignore the people watching you. Once you've mastered that, the rest gets easier as you go along. My situation may be different than yours because I believe those who kept me under surveillance were people in authority abusing their power. And, a private security firm, hired by a former investor who did not receive all of his investment back from my failed real estate business. I've seen obvious signs and exposed many people who followed me around. It was difficult to ignore them telling everyone I came in contact with that I'm public enemy numero uno, but I did it.

THE PROCESS

The process of overcoming being under surveillance takes prayer, patience and persistence because it does pay off. In addition to prayer, patience is key because you may never know when the people who are watching you will stop. Your process may be different and it may take something other than what works for me. I'm a man of a high level of faith so prayer works for me. Because I rely on prayer as a direct means of conversation with God, I have patience enough to wait to see my prayers answered. I pray for my enemies. I've learned to let patience have its perfect work. I'm persistent in moving forward with forging new paths. I forget those things which are behind and take hold of that which is ahead of me. I can't change the past, but I know that if I work hard taking new, positive steps forward, it will eventually pay off. You can do the same.

THE SUCCESS

Overcoming the setback of being under surveillance has many benefits including getting out from under someone else's thumb. I mentioned this same benefit in the chapter on being blacklisted because they are closely related. Not in all cases, but from my experiences where people were working hard to ruin any new relationships I worked hard to develop, getting out from under that kind of demonic, unforgiving, and destructive activity is a great benefit.

Another advantage is that you learn to be accountable to yourself and others by not letting anything take you off course and away from your mission, purpose and path of forging new, positive ground.

God gives His children numerous chances to correct behavior. He is patient throughout the process because He knows that change does not take place overnight. People are good by nature because God, who is always good, created us in His image. And because we're created in the image of God we are by nature, good. What causes us to change course and alter what is good in us by nature is sin. Sin is always bad. Once we've committed sin against God, or any crime that is not sin, against another human, we must be punished for it, learn the lesson therein, and correct the behavior that caused it. Once you've endured the test and accomplished the task, the success of overcoming being under surveillance will be evident and you will be a much better person by having gone through it.

THE SETBACK
~SABOTAGE~

In over 16 years in active ministry one of the most important things I've learned is that the devil is real. Sometimes, he can be used by God to bring bad things, bad events, bad people into your life. Like Job chapter one in the Bible describes, the devil may think he's being allowed to curse you but God's plan to bless you is at work all along.

During the past 18 years, I've lived through many situations where the devil was being used and was using people to sabotage many of the projects I was working on. It came in the form of giving false information to people I was working with, and a host of other tools he used to try and throw me off track. Remember, there is no truth in the devil so nothing he does is honest and forthright, even when he's allowed by God to touch your life. God places us in certain situations to mold us, shape us, remake us, strengthen us, and prepare us for something He wants us to do and He equips us for the journey. Without tests we have no testimony and without trials and tribulations we cannot be triumphant.

Sabotage is one of the most difficult setbacks I've had to learn to deal with in my life. Not because it's harder than anything else I've been through, but because of the very nature of things people do. The evil they do, you MUST forgive. And because you have to forgive, I suggest you also forget.

THE CHALLENGE

The challenge to overcome the setback of having everything you work to accomplish be sabotaged starts with being able to forgive and forget. This is not an easy thing to do, but you must summon the strength to be able to. Here are three reasons why:

(1) You are being sabotaged for a purpose.
The purpose may be because you are called into an area of ministry that the devil knows once you decide to walk in it, will tear down many strongholds he has built up.

(2) Hating you is not a hurdle it's a help.
God chastises those He loves, so the devil's hatred of you should be clear indication that something God is doing to bless your life is causing the devil a major headache.

(3) You exposing your past is testimony.
When someone else does it without you being involved, it's gossip. Only the devil will keep reminding you and telling others about your past to try and block blessings that God has laid out for your future.

If you believe God then you know that Romans 8:28 is the honest to God truth that, *"All things work together for the 'good' of those who love God, and are the called according to His purpose."* This scripture, is what helps me meet the challenge of having things I do sabotaged by the devil and by people. It's as simple as that.

THE PROCESS

The process of overcoming the actions of the devil and people doing things to sabotage what you do starts with being able to forgive and forget.

When I learned that people were sabotaging my projects, job interviews, relationships with other people, contracts, work on various projects, potential sales from customers, etc., I *felt* I had to do something. God wants us to be still, leave room for His wrath, and embrace His peace that passeth all understanding.

I didn't retaliate because I knew it would interfere with God's plan. Instead, I focused my efforts on continuing to pray, have patience, be persistent, knowing that it would eventually pay off. What I suggest you do is simple:

(1) Respond to negative information with positive results.
(2) React to negative circumstances with positive outcomes.
(3) Reply to negative people with positive statements.

In the process of you overcoming the setback of sabotage remember Matthew 5:44: *"Love your enemies, bless them that curse you, do good to them that hate you, and pray for them which despitefully use you and persecute you."* Use this scripture as your shield and buckler, and you shall have peace that passes all understanding, which guards your heart and your mind.

THE SUCCESS

Let me remind you that lying is the devil's native language and his actions are to steal, kill, and destroy (i.e. SABOTAGE) any and everything that God is trying to do to bless you.

(1) The more the devil steals from you...

The more you should be giving others too.

(2) The more the devil kills what you do...

The more you should be giving birth to something new.

(3) The more the devil destroys your plan...

The more you should be thanking God all you can.

One thing I've learned about having success after sabotage is that the devil is not interested in you or your life or who you are or what you do <u>unless</u> **you are a direct threat to him and his strongholds.**

If things in your life keep happening over and over and over again with seemingly no positive results or success, **it is because you are a major thorn in the devil's side and you should do all you can to help build up and edify the Body of Christ, the church and the ministry** in each and every way you possibly can.

Then and only then will you begin to see God's plan in your success.

PRAYER, PATIENCE & PERSISTENCE PAYS

Greetings,
I'm Pastor Keith...

If you're experiencing a setback in your life right now say these words

This Too Shall Pass

SuccessAfterSetback.com

THE SETBACK ⬐   THE CHALLENGE

Success
After
Setback

Chapter
Five

BOUNCING BACK

While gathering my thoughts and notes for this chapter, I thanked God for how Blessed I am. He's allowed me and helped me to bounce back from many adversities and setbacks I've had in my life. From numerous tragedies in my childhood and the resulting rebellion; the incarceration to correct behavior; to countless burned bridges and negative outcomes in personal and business relationships. I've leaned and depended on God to help me through each and every incident, situation and circumstance, and it worked out.

You can bounce back from each and every setback that occurs in your life; hurdle that gets placed in your path; circumstance that knocks you down; enemy that causes you pain; relationship that ends badly. You may come out of these a little worse for wear and a little weathered from the storm, but you can bounce back. Prayer, patience and persistence, eventually pays off, but getting through the process is the toughest part.

To bounce back from the variety of setbacks that occurred in my life I looked within to God's spirit that lives in me for the strength needed to overcome feelings that can usher you into a state of depression. Once I learned to master that, I made the commitment to myself and my family that I would get up, let God dust me off and place me back on the path He paved for me instead of any I would choose. It was my choices that caused me to veer off the path in the first place.

It took willingness on my part because God is able. He's able to do exceedingly above all that we ask or think. Having God on my side through each and every setback is more than I could ever ask for.

God is a forgiving, loving, understanding and restoring Father. He knows we're going to mess things up before we ever do. He created us. He knows we're prone to making mistakes before we ever do. His process to turn things around starts with confession, takes a step toward surrender, ushers in repentance, and is moved forward into restoration. All of this sits on a foundation of love, which it the tie that binds it all together.

Each setback is an often unexpected event that occurs in your life that when allowed to play itself out, without your interruption, can make you stronger once you've gone through the process of overcoming it. Most people only deal with one or two setbacks in their lifetime, but I've dealt with and overcome dozens. I had to come to the realization of why my life took such turns along the way. The only thing I can equate these setbacks to, is that because I'm called to pastor, witness to, and minister to the masses, that I needed the varied experiences to be able to relate to people and help them get through their situations.

The next 20 pages contain reminder quotes from me. I suggest you use them, or create your own, to help strengthen you along your journey. And I pray for success after your setbacks.

The Secret to Bouncing Back

is standing your ground
in spite of the adversity all around you.

Bouncing Back from Tragedy

Takes forgiving
whoever caused it.

Bouncing Back from Drug Use

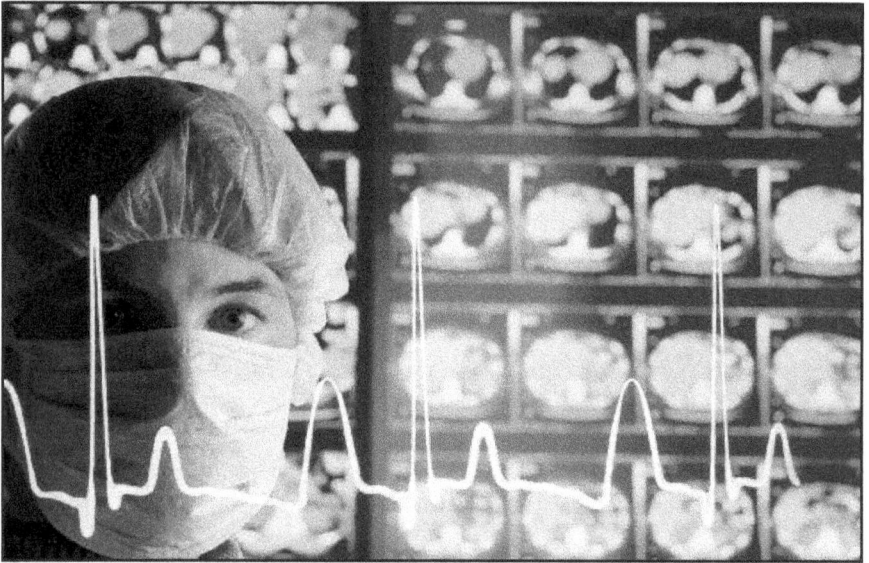

Takes realizing your body is a temple and living that way.

Bouncing Back from Drug Sales

Requires commitment to stop distributing a substance that can destroy lives.

Bouncing Back from Gang Affiliation

Takes the courage to walk away
in spite of any retaliation.

Bouncing Back from Fornication

Simply takes keeping yourself from sleeping with anyone you're not married to.

Bouncing Back from Lying

Only requires that you always tell the truth no matter the consequence.

Bouncing Back from Negative Outcomes

Takes building a buffer around yourself by delegating certain operations.

Bouncing Back from Felonies

Stars with correcting the behavior
that cause you to commit the crime.

Bouncing Back from Victims

Requires you to first forgive yourself, then never harm anyone ever again.

Bouncing Back from Enemies

Means forgiving anyone that harms you, as if it never happened.

Bouncing Back from Foreclosure

Just needs you to let go of the past house, so you can walk into your future home.

Bouncing Back from Lawsuits

Shows that you're willing to stand your ground and tell the truth about it.

Bouncing Back from Judgments

Means you're committed to paying anything you owe over a period of time.

Bouncing Back from Liens

Starts with making payment plans and sticking to them until paid.

Bouncing Back from Bankruptcy

Takes forging a new path with new income and renewed commitment.

Bouncing Back from Debt

Requires you to pay off existing debt and prudently manage new income.

Bouncing Back from Burned Bridges

Begins by repairing any bridges that can be, and making a commitment to build new ones.

Bouncing Back from Surveillance

Shows that you're willing to be accountable and able to withstand any type of scrutiny.

Bouncing Back from Sabotage

Takes forgiving those who do it,
and focusing on creating positives.

PRAYER, PATIENCE & PERSISTENCE PAYS

Greetings,
I'm Pastor Keith...

If you need additional help to get through your setback contact me.

keith@ SuccessAfterSetback.com

I look forward to helping you in whatever way God wills.

SuccessAfterSetback.com

BOOKS

I'm the author of dozens of books. Many of them I've self published. They cross several genres such as Faith, Inspiration, How-To, Business, Education, Technology, Romance, Relationships, Church Ministry, and Leadership Training.

My writing career began when I took a class in Journalism in 1987 at Chicago State University. During the course, I tried to land a job at a newspaper and was constantly told by editors that *'You need experience'*, as they brushed me off. My response was always *'How do you expect me to get experience if no one will give me an assignment!'*

Doors to write didn't open until 1991 when I moved to Minnesota.

Then, from 1992-1997 every single editorial door I knocked on opened to me. It blessed me to write dozens of feature articles and other stories for local papers.

Talk about Minnesota Nice!

These editors enabled me to write articles about and interview people like Maya Angelou, Dick Gregory, Lauren Green and many others. You can read many of the articles I've written at:

LessonsForLifeBooks.com/articles.pdf

Writing for newspapers transitioned into writing scripts and my first one was written and sent to Star Trek: The Next Generation. I'm a Trekkie, and proud of it. My script writing gained me valuable experience. In 1999 I used my writing skills to create a 200-page proposal to build and open a high school. It focused on basic standards emphasizing trade certification in two areas prior to graduation. It earned me a $1M annual contract with a district but the politics coupled with my questioning them green-stamping diplomas for kids who couldn't read pulled the rug out from under me months after opening. 30 staff, 225 students and their parents were affected.

2002 I wrote about the ordeal. It's titled: *Education The Right Way*. I looked for a literary agent and couldn't get one. I submitted my manuscript to dozens of publishers with nothing but form letter responses. I was approached by Vanity presses, but I couldn't afford the thousands they were asking for to do the book. I set it aside, kept writing, and put each manuscript I finished on the shelf. I committed myself to completing a book per/month for 10 years without formatting or editing, just writing, and I accomplished it.

In 2008 the editing process began. I queried editors but couldn't come to terms on their rates for the growing list of material I had compiled. I tried to edit myself but it was way too time consuming. Although I'm considered a fantastic writer, I'm not even close to being the best editor. I'm not objective when it comes to my own writing voice, so it's probably best that I don't edit my own work.

Since finishing numerous manuscripts, publishing many of them, 'finding my voice' and watching it mature throughout the process, to date I've written over 80 books. I publish many of my own books under my own company: Lessons For Life Books, Inc.

Launching the company and moving it forward by discovering our audience and market, has been and continues to be invaluable.

People often ask me about my favorite books. I have favorite books I've written, but my most favorite books by other authors include:

+ The Holy Bible
+ On Walden Pond
+ Rich Dad Poor Dad
+ The Audacity of Hope
+ Who Moved My Cheese
+ The Power of Positive Thinking
+ Dig Your Well Before You're Thirsty

There are many reasons that these books top the list of my favorites by other authors but amongst all the books I've ever read, these are by far the most beneficial and added volumes to my life in many ways. In addition to my own Lessons For Life Books publishing site, my books are available on many of the traditional book-buying websites and I pray that you enjoy reading them, as much as I love writing them.

BOOKSTORE

As the author of dozens of books on faith, inspiration, church and ministry, opening my own faith-based bookstore is a natural fit. There aren't many authors who have done this. In fact, only one other author in the Twin Cities area is known for his own bookstore, and as far as I know, it's not faith-based.

Although I fully embrace the eBook revolution as both an author and avid reader, I still wholeheartedly support small, cozy, community-based bookstores. Just like libraries are a necessity, I feel the same way about places that promote and sell books.

In 2013, I opened my first faith-based bookstore in St. Paul in a small community where there are two liquor stores and over half dozen bars within immediate walking distance. On top of that, four years prior to the store opening, a pastor and his family were run out of the same neighborhood after a cross was burned on their lawn.

God used me to make many positive changes in that neighborhood. It's typical for me to stand up to adversity by being a vessel to be placed on the front line against such hatred and racism.

My bookstore contains my books, at prices discounted from online. I feel if a customer will travel to come to the store they deserve to pay lower price. And I'm always welcome to see any customer.

Many of my bookstore locations are selected with ministry in mind.

The vision is to build faith-based bookstores in communities where there is a great need for them.

My bookstore is also a cafe`. It provides a warm, inviting and wonderful atmosphere for people who want to come and enjoy a cup of coffee, tea, cider, chai, mocha, espresso, cappuccino, and so on, as well as any one of our many pastries.

We host book clubs, author signings, poetry readings, group meetings, jewelry showcases, makeup parties, bridal showers, chess club, sports nights, video game tournaments, etc. The atmosphere in the store is designed to start conversations, play a game of chess, or connect with friends, family or associates.

As of the publication of this book, I'm hard at work researching, planning and focused on opening additional locations.

The ultimate goal may be to franchise the bookstores. However, as you can see from many of the chapters in this book, containing brief summaries of the myriad of setbacks that have cross my path, and hurdles that have been placed in front of me, that it makes me take any growth that God grants increase for, one location at a time.

One . location . at . a . time, and **Books 'N Tea** is well on its way.

OPENING YOUR OWN BOOKSTORE/CAFE`

Staring a new business is often difficult. Opening my own bookstore that doubles as a cafe, owned by the author of most of the books in the store, with faith as it's foundation, makes opening a new business even more difficult because of my past as well as opposition to Jesus.

If you're planning to open your own bookstore someday, whether it is a franchise of **Books 'N Tea** (my stores) or one of your own, here are many of the nuances I've learned that can help you, including:

+ Finding the right location
+ LONG TERM LEASE
+ Permits, inspections, licensing, etc.
+ People to interview, hire and train
+ Cleaning and maintenance contracts
+ Advertising and marketing materials
+ Beverage equipment and related water lines
+ Water Filters and other related devices
+ Furniture and other décor
+ Retail POS systems for cash and credit
+ Phones, music on-hold & other technology such as WI-FI
+ Cable TV [optional]
+ Coffee, Tea, Beverage and Food Selections and condiments
+ Beverage products, (hot/cold cups, mugs, drink mixers, etc.)
+ Paper products, (napkins, toilet paper, paper towels, etc.)
+ Trash bins and service

+ Books and other product inventory

+ Window lettering and other signage

+ Fire extinguishers, smoke alarms

+ First-aid and other safety equipment

+ Labor signage, time clock

+ Power and outlets capable of handling all the equipment, systems, and customers when they come in to use their laptops, etc.

+ Adequate and functional bathroom facilities

+ Security system and monitoring service

+ Product displays, shelving and other racks

+ Menu boards, pricing and customer brochures, coupons and punch cards

+ Dishwashing and sanitizing system

+ Neon open and coffee signs

+ Sandwich board and other outdoor marketing signage

+ Exterior landscaping, furniture and other décor

Many of these things may be different for you depending on your location, and may not apply to your business model, décor and a host of other variables. Again, I'm building stores because it's part of my ministry. I'm the author of many books and I needed a platform and place to showcase my books, tea and beverage brand, etc. Thus, opening stores is a natural fit for me and a new notch on my success after setback belt.

If you need help in any way, email Keith@BooksandTea.net

THE CAFE˙ SIDE OF THINGS

A recent article (Jan. 2014) in a major national magazine, it features the growth and popularity of the bookstore/cafes˙ concept. You can see the "Sit and Sip" article at BooksandTea.net/sitandsiparticle.pdf

As the author of many faith-based and inspirational books, I needed a platform and place to launch this part of the ministry God has blessed me with and entrusted to me.

Books 'N Tea are my bookstore/cafés where we also serve coffee, chai, cappuccino, espresso, mochas, packaged and fresh pastries, etc. The store features my own tea and beverage brand, but also carries products from other manufacturers to round out our inventory.

On the coffee shop side of things, we are traditional but again, our foundation is faith. The stores carry inspirational books I've written, along with products that promote having a relationship with God through His Son Jesus, from various perspectives including theologian, lay-member, pastoral, etc. Most of my books are practical in the sense that I'm the living witness whose experiences God uses to inspire me to write them down as testimony to help others.

That's one major difference about us. And many other differences can be identified through a basic understanding of our core mission, vision, values and objectives, as well as the locations we select.

Many other differences can be identified through a basic understanding of our core mission, vision, values and objectives. We are different in our approach and unique in our concept. Our key principles, building blocks and anticipated outcomes are different. Such as:

Traditional coffee-shops roast coffee.
We sell prepackaged coffee.

Traditional coffee-shops typically don't sell books.
We sell my books as well as help other authors sell theirs.

Traditional coffee-shops limit their tea selections.
We sell my tea brand as well as products from other manufacturers.

Traditional coffee-shops aren't faith-based.
We are faith-based but respect everyone's journey.

Traditional coffee-shops aren't a ministry for the owner.
Books 'N Tea is a part of my ministry.

Traditional coffee-shops don't host book signings.
Part of our mission is to host regular book signings.

Traditional coffee-shops aren't owned by authors.
I'm an author; I own Books 'N Tea.

These are just a few of the things that differentiate Books 'N Tea from traditional coffee shops. There are many other variables that make us unique including our branding and packaging, my books, my tea and beverage brand, products I'm working to patent, etc.

One of the most glaring differences is that when people come in needing help, we do our best to reach out and assist in any way we can. That's rare in any traditional coffee shop.

There have and continue to be several situations that our customers have come in and requested assistance with. And, customers who know I'm a pastor [plug: Gospel and Grace Christian Church], often come in seeking advice, prayer, and just a listening ear.

Often, because I'm the owner, customers will come in when they see I'm in the stores and hope for an opportunity to talk to me. Many of them know the various experiences I've had, both good and bad, and want to talk to someone who's been through what they may be currently experiencing.

This is by far my favorite reason for opening Books 'N Tea because it gives me an opportunity to be a living witness, and minister to people from all walks of life with all sorts of problems.

With all I've been through in my life, I have a plethora of testimonies from which to draw.

A NEW CD

In 2013 I presided over the funeral of my nephew. I was one of two pastors. He was one of my sister's sons. He passed away in his sleep at age 26. Several hundred members of our family and several hundred of his friends were in attendance.

At the funeral I sang one of my favorite Gospel songs titled: '*The Blood That Jesus Shed For Me.*' Many of my family members were seeing me in the pulpit for the first time, and many of them had not ever seen or heard me sing. When I sang, it brought many of my family members to tears.

I also shared some of my testimony with those in attendance, as many of them had no idea and had yet to see me working in the ministry.

I presided over the burial alone, as the other pastor left after the funeral to attend another event. As the crowd of 150 of our family and his friends followed me from the hertz, I read scriptures and other sayings as I led the processional to the burial site.

My prayer centered on the hearts of the people who came to the burial site to see my nephew laid to rest. I prayed that God would heal their hearts but to also touch them in a way that would let them look at their own lives before it becomes too late.

Prior to becoming a pastor, I served in the ministry under my pastor for 12 years at a Baptist church in downtown Minneapolis.

In that dozen years of service, I've participated in numerous funerals both as Head Deacon and as the right hand to my pastor. It was often my responsibility or my pastor's request to meet with the family prior to the service, even down to the details such as designing the programs. I was well trained and learned many things from my pastor's leadership in this area.

My experiences consist of many years teaching and giving talks to many groups. Some of those teachings I've turned into free material others use, books that contain templates, free tracts, and so on.

While at the church my wife and I served as worship leaders for many years. I sang many solos and led our worship team in song. But what made me want to take these varied experience and use some of it to release a CD? Simple: God.

This year, while being obedient in a lengthy Fast, God placed it on my heart to put my varied experiences, teachings, and other material into audio in the form of Podcasts. I was obedient. Now on our church website [GospelandGraceChurch.org] visitors can listen to or download dozens of my Podcasts on a variety of subjects.

One of those subjects is Prayer and that's where we come to the CD.

Again, during a lengthy Fast, while preparing some of the Podcasts on Prayer, God laid it on my heart to take some of the prayers, and a handful of songs, compile them into a CD, and release it.

A Pastor's Prayer
The Prayers and Petitions of a Pastor

The CD was born. I was obedient.

To move forward with the assignment I contacted a great friend of mine who owns a recording studio. He is a brother I've been in fellowship with; attended church with for a dozen years; and sang acapella with at a nursing home, after conducting a funeral at the church we worshipped at together. I went into his studio, laid down the tracks, and God took my willingness, added it to His able, and did the rest. The CD is planned for release quite soon.

Given what I've been through and the many setbacks that have plagued my life, every new book, CD, and store that God allows me to publish, produce, or open, I CONSIDER A BLESSING that mere words cannot express thanks enough for.

I have a natural vibrato, but I never saw releasing my own CD in any part of my future. I thank God that He saw it because He ordered my steps to walk into it as if it was right there in front of me all along. Again, given the setbacks, I find that truly amazing.

A NEW CHURCH

If you look back into chapter one under the section on Fornication, you'd see that In 1979 my dad handed me my fist Bible. From that moment, the devil got super busy trying to keep me from ever waling into my calling. I knew I was different. Set aside to be used by God for His Greatness and His Glory. But circumstances kept me distracted and away from God's will for 17 long years.

In November of 1980, the day my dad passed, I knew I was called to the ministry. I didn't understand why, how, or any of the logistics, but I knew from sitting in Sunday school and mass for many years before that day, I wasn't retaining all the verses of scripture I read, and sayings such as the Apostle's Creed, just because I have a sharp mind. I knew there was a reason and I was right.

In 1997, when I walked back into the church for the first time in 17 years, God embraced me as if I had returned home because I had. God waited, patiently, for me to come to terms with the deaths of my mom and dad and seek His face for the love, guidance, and direction, that I longed for.

In June 2012 God blessed me to formally register
Gospel and Grace Christian Church
The planning had been taking place since 2009, but God still had work to do on me and my heart just to prepare me for the planting.

My preparation for the assignment to pastor a church began the day I walked back into a church in 1997 for the first time in 17 years. I don't know how it happened, but within days, I was called in to the pastor's office and offered the post at his right hand.

I was new to that church. The pastor didn't formally know me. But God saw fit to place me in the position I needed to be in to start training and preparation to one day stand in similar shoes.

Over 16 years in active ministry I've attended conferences, conventions, seminary, taught classes, led ministries, and served in numerous leadership roles at two churches under two pastors.

Over 16 years, I served under two pastors. Rev. Agnew in Minneapolis for 12 1/2 years from 1997-2009; and Pastor Claiborn in Bloomington for 2 1/2 years from 2009-2011. God gave me the vision to design a church for Him and it's a beautiful campus, which will be built by God's hand someday. From the day I joined his church, I informed Pastor Claiborn that I would most definitely and eventually be following God's call to plant a church.

Being under the leadership of these two great men of God, I learned many valuable lessons and I am truly honored and grateful to them both for their love, patience, teaching, prayers, and too many other things to list, including their willingness to put up with me. Under their pastoral covering I served in many leadership roles.

Under Pastor Agnew	Under Pastor Claiborn
The Pastor's right hand	Produced 1 hour church TV show
Led the Deacons	Redesigned/Printed church bulletins
Led Sunday School Teachers	Redesigned/Printed annual programs
Taught Adult Sunday School	Trained members in graphic design
Designed flyers, banners, cards	Trained members in website design
Printed programs, posters	Designed flyers, banners, cards
Installed technology systems	Designed/Printed programs, posters
Designed new church building	Upgraded/Repaired computers
Programmed the web site	Redesigned the church web site
Published the church newsletter	Redesigned the church newsletter
Published the membership book	Redesigned the member handbook
Published the church cookbook	Designed new church logo
Designed the church database	Designed YouTube Channel
Gave numerous presentations	Directed Brotherhood Choir
Chaired many successful ministries	Developed a church info DVD
Worked to expand a prison ministry	Developed a marketing campaign
Worked to develop a TV ministry	Designed new church campus

These experiences were invaluable. In part, it is how God molded, shaped, reshaped, gifted, trained, educated, empowered, and prepared me to plant and pastor a church. Each of the experiences helps me on this incredible journey. To God, and to these two men of God, I thank you for your unwavering and unfailing love, without which, I could not have come this far. More about my journey is in my book titled: *Pastors Are Not Perfect*.

Success
After
Setback

Chapter
Six

BUILDING NEW BRIDGES

I've been through many trials and tribulations in my life. Many of them were self-inflicted, but all of them helped me mature in some way. Because I burned so many bridges across various facets of personal and business relationships, I've learned many lessons that are invaluable to others, which is why I share my testimonies.

As I've referenced and outlined in other chapters, focusing on the fallout behind bridges you've burned takes too much time and energy. Instead, let prayer, patience, and persistence take the reins, and it will eventually pay off. Stop focusing on past that you can't change, and instead put time, energy and resources into building new bridges.

Building new bridges takes focus and effort. In my situation, I focused on writing books, building a publishing company, opening bookstore/cafés, and creating a tea and beverage brand. Each one of these is time consuming. Combined they take up more than enough of my time to keep me from letting my thoughts drift off to my past. I also had to realize that at some point I would be thrust back into situations where people from my past would hear my name, and see me working on another project. I had to learn not to walk in fear of reprisal, or fear of them telling anyone I'm currently working with that I had a failed project or two in the past. I stay the course, remain focused and let God deal with my past and the people in it. You can do the exact the same thing.

Building new bridges means earning new trust. This isn't always easy if the bridges you burned in your past were exposed publicly, meaning over the TV news or in the newspaper. My fall was public, and so was the fallout. I went to jail and out came the cameras.

It took a lot for me to be still, keep quiet, and let God handle the situations through His loving arms of forgiveness and the armor He wrapped me in for protection.

+ Each circumstance I faced, I learned many lessons.
+ Each struggle I endured, made me stronger.
+ Each person that lost money investing in any of my projects, I had to apologize, pray for their forgiveness, and move forward believing that God would bring healing and peace, restitution and restoration.

Aside from the often overwhelming feelings of sorrow and guilt that came whenever I thought about being the reason investors lost money, I stay focused on the new tasks, new bridges, new relationships, and new paths. Investors were not the only ones affected when I burned bridges, my family was also. They had to face the public scrutiny as well as the judgment. The hardest part for them was dealing with the fallout of me having to go to jail to pay penance for what I'd done. Although I did the crime, in effect, they did time too. They were without my income; my guidance; my leadership; my protection, my presence, and many other things.

The vast majority of the men I met in prison didn't have families to return to. They lost support from and often access to their families typically because of the type of crime they committed. More often than not, just because they committed a crime regardless of type.

My family's support is why I work so hard to forge new paths, build new trust, and become a much better person and leader than I was in the past. With each new day I see that it will take time but it's working. Given what I've been through, and put others through, I couldn't ask for much more success after setback than that.

In the chapter '*Burned Bridges*' I referenced a few things I suggest to start building new bridges. They include:

+ Trusting God.
+ Swallowing pride.
+ Delegating duties.

There are more, but when you're willing to do these things God will step in and order your steps to do so.

When His purpose is in you He is passionate about helping you.

TAKING RISKS

Taking risks has been part of my life since my early adulthood. It's something I learned to do as part of being a black male, with visions and dreams, high hopes and major aspirations. While I know that everyone has hopes and aspirations, I always knew mine were different somehow. I always used to hear, 'No Risk No Reward', so I knew that in order for me to receive any kind of reward, whether earthly or Heavenly, I would have to take risk to do so. I knew very early in my life that there is a distinct difference between earthly rewards and Heavenly ones. I didn't know to what depth yet, but I did recognize that there is a difference.

Many people never take risk. For example, there are millions of people who are satisfied with just going to work 9 to 5 everyday, under the same routine, year after year, with their only hope being a retirement party and possibly a gold-plated watch after two or three decades of working to make someone else wealthy. My wife was one of those people. For the past 20 years, she was a Director for a large nonprofit. She retired in December 2013. They gave her a party and a gift, but that's it! After working 20 years in the same routine, she was at a loss for what to do next.

Some think this routine is the most stable, but I don't believe Jesus came to earth and died for our sins so we could work on someone else's agenda all your life. My wife is 9 to 5; I'm a total risk-taker.

God has her life in His hands, so my wife will be just fine. Many who retire, often end up becoming depressed because the routine they knew and walked in for so long, is no longer the focus of their life, so they start to give up on life, and often end up leaving this life.

I was called to the Ministry at age 17. I realized it the day my dad gave me my first Bible. I knew I was different. I thought different. I acted different. I cared about things different. I prayed even though I was never taught how to pray.

Heavenly reward is eternal. I knew back then that the only way for me to achieve reward from Heaven I had to take risk and follow Jesus in the way He walked, talked, acted, reacted, and lived life.

I knew that risk meant stepping out on faith and letting God use me to plant or pastor a church, and various ministries. However, the day my dad passed, I got angry, walked away from God, and the church. Through my own selfish rebellion I didn't return for 17 years. God is able to comfort and heal. I was too angry to take the risk and let Him. I regret this decision to this day.

Taking risk in business is different. I've taken risks to start businesses; invest in others, etc. If any business isn't successful there's usually some financial fallout. Again, no risk no reward. Without risk there's typically no type of reward. When risk is taken, and there is success, the rewards are often very satisfying and 'rewarding'.

I've learned that taking a level of risk in business is not much different than taking risk to let God use me in the ministry. Both take willingness. Without being willing to take risk in business, there's no earthly reward. Without being willing to take a risk and let God use you in the ministry, there's no Heavenly reward. The glaring difference between these two is that the earthly reward is temporary; the Heavenly one is eternal. I've taken risks to start:

+ a relationship, which has lasted 30 years in marriage
+ a family, which has produced two daughters and grandkids
+ a computer company
+ a printing business
+ a school
+ a consulting firm
+ a publishing company
+ a bookstore/café'
+ many books
+ many nonprofits

In each of these ventures, I had to be willing to sow the seed of risk to have any possibility of reaping any harvest of reward. Any business I ever started that did not have God at the forefront, or Him in the purpose, mission, vision, goals and objectives, failed. The opposite is true with businesses I've started with ministry and mission as their focus. They continue to succeed, and positively impact the lives of many people. Therefore, follow God. Take risk with God. Although the process may not meet your timeline or expectation, rest assured that you will win and be rewarded each and every single time.

SUPPORT GROUPS

I wrote *Success After Setback* to share my testimony, so you can learn from my experiences and not make the same mistakes. Overcoming any difficult situation in your life takes support. It doesn't matter what form help comes in, just that is does come. I'm a huge advocate and proponent of support groups. I'm a firm believer that connecting with a group of people who have the same or similar experiences as you, can offer invaluable insight into getting past whatever it is you are going through.

Support groups can help you deal with Tragedy, Drug Addiction, Drug Sales, Gang Affiliation, Fornication, Lying, Negative Outcomes, Felonies, Forgiving those who won't forgive you, Enemies, Foreclosure, Lawsuits, Judgments, Liens, Bankruptcy, Debt, Burned Bridges, Being Blacklisted, Being under surveillance, Bouncing Back, Building New Bridges, Taking Risk, and a host of other issues, problems, circumstances, setbacks, and situations that we go through and experience at different times in our lives.

Support groups are a dynamic way to release what you've been holding on to. Being in a setting that gives you a platform to speak freely about something you did, or something that was done to you, without being judged, ridiculed, or retaliated against, is a tremendous step forward. Being in a support group takes participation, commitment and honesty.

Your participation in a support group doesn't mean you're any less than anyone else. I had to learn that. I realized that I'm actually just as good or better than anyone who'd look down on me because I've done wrong. And, I'm smart enough to be willing to step up and ASK FOR HELP!

Your participation in any support group requires commitment to see it through. Don't think for one moment that you can just go once, get a few answers then never go back. It doesn't work that way.

What does work, is committing yourself to the process of healing, and deliverance, and taking the steps necessary to overcome whatever setback you've experienced.

The most important and vital part of participating in or committing to a support group is to be honest. You must be honest with God; Honest with yourself; and honest with those in the group so that through your experiences, you can do two things:

1. Get help
2. Be helpful

You are there to freely give, whereby you freely receive. Do so, and you will benefit greatly. Again, thanks for taking the time to listen to my story. I pray you enjoy reading it as much as I loved writing it.

148

DO YOU WANT TO BE AN AUTHOR?

If you've written a book and need help getting published contact me.

Greetings,
I'm Pastor Keith...

keith@ LessonsForLifeBooks.com

I'm an Author/Expert with many published books

LessonsForLifeBooks.com

COMING SOON
A new CD by
Pastor Keith Hammond

A Pastor's Prayer

The Prayers and Petitons of a Pastor

Pastor Keith Hammond

Look for it online or order it at GospelandGraceChurch.org

COMING SOON
Podcasts by
Pastor Keith Hammond

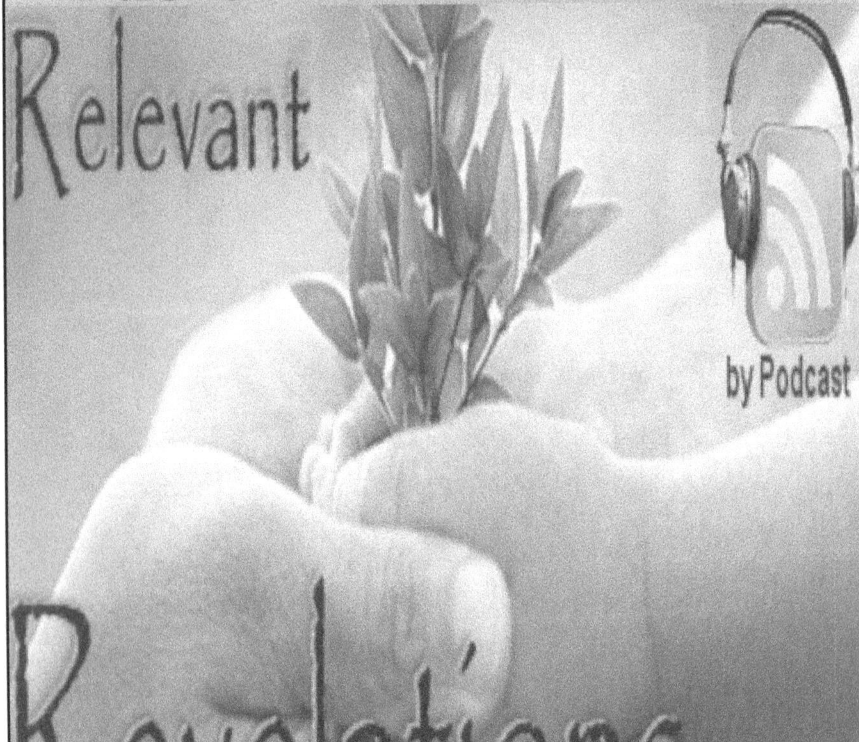

Relevant

by Podcast

Revelations

Listen or download
them at
GospelandGraceChurch.org

LET ME REMIND YOU SO YOU CAN TELL OTHERS

Greetings,
I'm Pastor Keith...

"If God waited on people to become perfect before He anointed them to preach, teach, lead or minister, there would never be anyone worthy, and the work would never get done...

God uses willing vessels, with weaknesses, so His strength, power, and anointing, can shine through, and He can get the glory!"

SuccessAfterSetback.com

SUMMARY PAGES

What tragedy have you experienced?

How did it set you back?

How did you turn that into success?

Share your testimony at SuccessAfterSetback.com

What did drug use do to your life?

How did it set you back?

How did you turn that into success?

Share your testimony at SuccessAfterSetback.com

Have you sold drugs in the past?

How did it set you back?

How did you turn that into success?

Share your testimony at SuccessAfterSetback.com

Were you a member of a gang?

How did it set you back?

How did you turn that into success?

Share your testimony at SuccessAfterSetback.com

Has fornication plagued you?

How did it set you back?

How did you turn that into success?

Share your testimony at SuccessAfterSetback.com

SUMMARY PAGES

What lies have you told?

How did it set you back?

How did you turn that into success?

Share your testimony at SuccessAfterSetback.com

Have negative outcomes been a problem?

How did it set you back?

How did you turn that into success?

Share your testimony at SuccessAfterSetback.com

Are you a felon?

How did it set you back?

How did you turn that into success?

Share your testimony at SuccessAfterSetback.com

Is your past littered with victims?

How did it set you back?

How did you turn that into success?

Share your testimony at SuccessAfterSetback.com

Do you have any enemies?

How did it set you back?

How did you turn that into success?

Share your testimony at SuccessAfterSetback.com

SUMMARY PAGES

Have you lost a home through foreclosure?

How did it set you back?

How did you turn that into success?

Share your testimony at SuccessAfterSetback.com

Has anyone ever sued you?

How did it set you back?

How did you turn that into success?

Share your testimony at SuccessAfterSetback.com

Do you have any judgments against you?

How did it set you back?

How did you turn that into success?

Share your testimony at SuccessAfterSetback.com

Is a lien standing in your way?

How did it set you back?

How did you turn that into success?

Share your testimony at SuccessAfterSetback.com

Have you ever filed bankruptcy?

How did it set you back?

How did you turn that into success?

Share your testimony at SuccessAfterSetback.com

SUMMARY PAGES

What amount of debt have you overcome?

How did it set you back?

How did you turn that into success?

Share your testimony at SuccessAfterSetback.com

Are bridges burning behind you?

How did it set you back?

How did you turn that into success?

Share your testimony at SuccessAfterSetback.com

Have you ever been blacklisted?

How did it set you back?

How did you turn that into success?

Share your testimony at SuccessAfterSetback.com

Does anyone have you under surveillance?

How did it set you back?

How did you turn that into success?

Share your testimony at SuccessAfterSetback.com

Has anyone ever sabotaged your progress?

How did it set you back?

How did you turn that into success?

Share your testimony at SuccessAfterSetback.com

CLOSING THOUGHTS

Growth requires gall.

Have the gall to get up after being knocked down.

Audacity requires action.

Have the audacity to achieve when the odds are against you.

Persistence pays.

Have the persistence to proceed when every door closes in your face.

Patience waits on progress.

Have the patience to remember God's promises when you're in a place of darkness and can't see His light anywhere.

-oo-

I subscribe to the theology of "Do what you have to do until you can do better." This philosophy means that you volunteer until you get a job. Keep knocking on doors until one opens, keep going until you reach your destination, work a job but build a career, etc.

Without tests you would not have testimonies.

Without trials and tribulations you could not be triumphant.

...Thanks for listening

Pastor Keith Hammond

WILLING AND ABLE WORK TOGETHER
If you're willing, God is able.

Lessons For Life Books
PUBLISHERS
LESSONSFORLIFEBOOKS.COM

www.ingramcontent.com/pod-product-compliance
Lightning Source LLC
Chambersburg PA
CBHW052009090426
42741CB00008B/1616

* 9 7 8 1 9 3 8 5 8 8 5 5 6 *